More
DUMB
Things
Churches
Do

More DUMB Things Churches Do

{ *And New Stategies for Avoiding Them* }

Philip Wiehe and Linda McFadden

Morehouse Publishing

An imprint of Church Publishing Incorporated
Harrisburg – New York

Unless otherwise noted, the Scripture quotations contained herein are from the New Revised Standard Version Bible, copyright © 1989 by the Division of Christian Education of the National Council of Churches of Christ in the U.S.A. Used by permission. All rights reserved

Morehouse Publishing, 4775 Linglestown Road, Harrisburg, PA 17112

Morehouse Publishing, 445 Fifth Avenue, New York, NY 10016

Morehouse Publishing is an imprint of Church Publishing Incorporated.

Cover design by Corey Kent

Library of Congress Cataloging-in-Publication Data

Wiehe, Philip.
More dumb things churches do and new strategies for avoiding them /
Philip Wiehe and Linda McFadden.
p. cm.
Includes bibliographical references.
ISBN 978-0-8192-2258-9 (pbk.)
1. Church management. I. McFadden, Linda. II. Title.
BV652.W532 2009
254--dc22
2008042509

(ISBN 978-0-8192-2258-9)

Printed in the United States of America

09 10 11 12 13 14   10 9 8 7 6 5 4 3 2 1

Contents

Acknowledgments

When people talked to Philip after reading *Ten Dumb Things Churches Do,* they marveled over how accurately he had described their own parishes. At that point Philip calculated that he had had contact with about fifty parishes in the course of his career.

It is relatively easy to name the churches with which we have had contact in the past seven years, but we won't name them; they know who they are. However, we do want to thank them for all they have taught us. They have generated some wonderful and not so wonderful illustrations for this book. What they all have in common is a good sense of humor—we think. So, thank you!

Introduction

Now there are varieties of gifts, but the same Spirit; and there are varieties of services, but the same Lord; and there are varieties of activities, but it is the same God who activates all of them in everyone. To each is given the manifestation of the Spirit for the common good.

—1 Corinthians 12:4–7

This book arises from the premise that all Christians are called to participate in the continual renewal of the Body of Christ. As Paul says in 1 Corinthians 12:4–7, we believe that the Holy Spirit is at work in all of us to "make all things new" in the church, thereby enabling all of the ministries of the Body of Christ.

This ongoing task of renewing and re-energizing the church is not easy, however, for the Body is inclined to resist change. Still, God calls us to embody and to renew the Body of Christ, wherever and whenever we find ourselves. In our case, this means in the United States of America in the twenty-first century. This book is about that process of renewal. Specifically, it suggests some preliminary answers to the question: *How do we consciously embody God's presence in this time and place without getting in the way of the Spirit's ongoing work of renewal?*

To address this question, we must candidly describe the context in which renewal takes place. We do not intend to indulge in hand-wringing over the distressing decline in membership of our established mainline churches over the past half century. Rather, to borrow a metaphor from golf, we propose to play the ball where it lies, and the ball lies in the rough. (Admittedly we allude to golf with misgiving, as this is a sport about which we know very little.) The "rough" that constitutes the context of the church is post-modern, post-Christian contemporary American society. It is widely recognized that the social structures that once made church attendance the norm in most communities have vanished. We need not reiterate historical and sociological factors that are well documented elsewhere. Given our present circumstances, the pressing question that arises for the church is: What do churches do now?

To return to the metaphorical golf course, one possibility is to "take a mulligan" and throw the ball out into the middle of the fairway. In other words, we could just cut ourselves off from the history and traditions of our past and invent a new kind of church to fit the post-modern post-Christian world—a consumer's church for a consumer's world, with programs customized with the assistance of demographic and marketing studies. The many non-denominational mega-churches offering a smorgasbord of programs catering to thousands of members are examples of this approach. An alternative would be to start a house church with a handful of like-minded individuals, using readings from the Bible (or whatever the group regards as sacred texts). Many types of alternative churches are taking shape, growing, flourishing, and dying all the time.

This book focuses on those who chose a different path. Our task here is not to invent a new model of church, but "to play the ball in the rough where it lies," drawing on our best prayerful and creative selves.

The fact is that Jesus did not give us detailed instructions about how to be the church. Matthew 16:19 reports that Jesus gave Peter the keys to heaven and hell, an act that some traditions view as the precedent for a hierarchical priesthood. In the Great Commission (Matthew 28:19–20) Jesus instructs his disciples to go out and "make disciples of all nations." But again, Jesus did not tell us exactly how to go about this task, and, unfortunately, literal interpretations of his mandate to make everyone a disciple have possibly caused as much harm as good in the world.

What we have in lieu of an instruction manual for the church is a set of stories. These stories are of two types: Jesus' parabolic teachings, which are often brilliant in their ability to reveal truth on many levels, and narratives of his life and ministry. Both the stories that Jesus told and the stories about what he did provide a wealth of material about how to be the church, but clearly it's not easy to convert these rich narratives into an instruction manual for the church treasurer. Trying to use the parables of Jesus as the instruction book for the church is about as practical as using Moby Dick as an instruction manual for marine navigation.

Perhaps the single most helpful instruction we have from Jesus about how to be the Body of Christ is his post-Resurrection directive to Peter: "Feed my sheep" (John 21:15–17). Typically, for him, Peter does not immediately grasp what Jesus means, so Jesus has to repeat his instruction three times. Peter preferred tangible stuff like walking on water or building mountaintop shelters for numinous beings. If he were around today, Peter might be a very enthusiastic head of the building and grounds committee. We are behaving like Peter any time we try to equate ministry only with concrete, physical tasks. The lack of an instruction manual for the church leaves us in Peter's sandals, trying to figure out what Jesus meant by "feed my sheep."

Peter wasn't the only disciple who couldn't immediately grasp what Jesus wanted. According to John's gospel, Mary Magdalene was the first disciple to see Jesus after his Resurrection. She does not at first recognize Jesus when he appears to her (John 20:1–10), but when he calls her name, she recognizes his voice and reaches out to embrace him. Before she can touch him, however, Jesus cautions her, "Do not cling to me." Mary Magdalene wanted him to stick around, and the truth is, so do we.

Who was Jesus, anyhow, and why can't we pin him down? We submit that Christians' continued attempts to codify, define, and otherwise neutralize mystery—in other words, to cling to Jesus—have created problems for the church from the beginning. One obvious example is the array of theological understandings of what happens to bread and wine in the Eucharist arising from various Christian traditions. Jesus himself gave us no instruction on this; he simply spoke words derived from the Jewish seder blessings. The question of whether the bread and wine miraculously become his body or whether the whole thing is metaphorical has triggered major disputes over liturgical practice among Christians for a long time.

The desire to cling to Jesus may also help to explain the church's persistent impulse to erect monumental edifices to house our worship. Perhaps the encoded message of massive ecclesiastical structures is: *the more solid the building, the more firm can be our faith.* Unfortunately, the architectural forms of previous centuries may not be appropriate for twenty-first century ministries. For example, they are costly to build and maintain, they are not energy efficient, and they are so inflexible for other uses that they usually sit empty all week. Too often we permit our church real estate to become an expensive accumulation of stuff that limits, defines, encloses, and gets in the way of our faith. (Richard Giles has covered this topic well in his book *Re-pitching the Tent*[1].) As in our architecture, so also in our theology, we seek to cling to Jesus, accruing layer upon layer of definition of Jesus and never discarding anything that no longer works. We need to discern what is no longer necessary or no longer works well, lest the church topple beneath the accumulated weight of centuries. The tricky part is to edit our traditions and practices *judiciously*. Choosing what to keep from our traditions is an important task facing every congregation and each denomination.

The difficulty of this undertaking can be attested by anyone who has attempted to teach the Nicene Creed to a confirmation class. The Nicene Creed was created 1700 years ago by a group of male church leaders who were trying to define the faith over against competing versions of Christianity that were labeled as heresies. Their particular concern was to nail down the relationships among the persons of the Trinity. The theological subtleties of the Holy Trinity are not the most compelling part of the faith life of most Christians today, yet many churches continue to say this creed every Sunday. Wouldn't it make more sense to affirm the important bits of our faith by saying some words we clearly understand? We have heard clergy introduce the Nicene Creed as the Nicene "symbol" or the "ancient creed," as a way of putting some space between the text and ourselves. It is no wonder that many on the journey of faith have quit the system of "official" Christianity in favor of starting or attending churches with no denominational connection, hence no allegiance to the layers of tradition accrued over centuries.

To summarize our situation, then, the ministers of today—that is to say, all of us Christians—have come along at a time when the traditions, models for ministry, Christology, liturgical theology, and all the rest of it is up for grabs, and there is no instruction from the Master other than "feed my sheep."

Feed my sheep. What does that mean for contemporary urban and suburban dwelling Americans? While shepherd and sheep may still be commonplace in parts of Palestine and other agrarian societies, most of our knowledge of sheep is limited to glimmers of metaphorical insight we have gleaned from scripture: sheep aren't very bright and unless somebody keeps an eye on them, they may wind up lost. But even non-agrarian, car-driving, mall-shopping people can understand that Jesus' message is first and foremost about relationships. When all is said and done, all the parables are about relationships of God with people and people with one another. Jesus' teachings may not give us much help with the nuts and bolts of running the church, but they are a simple set of instructions on how to get along with each other: love one another and forgive one another, even your enemies.

So ministry is not so much about the nature of sheep as it is about *the relationship of the shepherd to the sheep.* If Jesus' message is primarily about relationships, then the imperative "feed my sheep" describes the relationship between people and pastor (which still means "shepherd"). The pastor's job is to nourish the congregation and enable the members of the congregation to nourish one another. Through preaching and teaching, worship and prayer, listening and counseling, the pastor offers nourishment to the congregation and teaches by example how people in the church (the "flock") can nourish one another. It's easy for a pastor to forget this simple mandate. While forming committees, fixing the furnace, and printing the Sunday bulletin may at one moment or another seem urgent, these activities can distract us from the primary task of providing nourishment for the people. Jesus said, "Feed my sheep," not, "Build my sheep a barn." If we take the metaphor too literally, the pastor may end up doing everything, including being a rescuer of lost causes. In truth, "feed my sheep" suggests that we are all shepherds for one another. The ongoing renewal of the church proceeds from that reciprocally nurturing relationship.

As we attempt to be the Body of Christ in the twenty-first century, we need to avoid the hazards of either oversimplifying the faith or clinging too tightly to a fixed notion of Jesus. We must also recognize that we cannot retreat to a nostalgic version of church based on idealized childhood experiences or to a romantic view of the church as a happy family. Further, being the Body of Christ in the twenty-first century requires mature understanding of our place as believers in a world that is in the throes of violent confrontation between non-believers and fanatically intolerant believers. The global village envisioned by Marshall McLuhan more than forty years ago is here. The world simply does not have room for absolutists who require everyone to conform to their way of understanding God (or anything else). And as for the "happy family," we still have a 50 percent divorce rate in the U.S. and are seeing the emergence of new models of the nuclear family by way of single parents and gay and lesbian couples. If a congregation wants to be a "happy family," it had better be open to a variety of family structures and dynamics.

The words of the Gospel remain the same but the context is always changing. Today, living as we do in a global village, we see and hear Jesus' message differently than did people in earlier centuries who lived in agrarian villages or industrial cities. The emphasis on a salvation connected to notions of an undefined future in another plane of reality—heaven and hell, in other words—is giving way to an understanding of salvation as reconciliation that connects to building the Reign of God here and now.

The good news in this is that at this precise moment in time we have an incredible opportunity to shape the church that is struggling to be the Body of Christ. Today, clergy and laity have the challenge and the opportunity of trying to re-form and renew the church from within. This book is about that effort.

Diagnosing Dysfunction

Dumb Things Churches Do
Diagnostic Test (DTCDDT)

Search your heart and honestly, before God, answer the following questions. If you accumulate more than twenty points before answering all of the questions, forget about the rest of it and GET HELP!

1. After a church meeting of any kind, is there another informal meeting in the parking lot that seems more important than the official one?
   Yes = 1 point

2. Do you know (or care) what your church's mission statement is?
   No = 1 point

3. Is there talk of solving an existing problem by "restructuring"?
   Yes = 2 points

4. Do the pastor and lay leaders ignore your suggestions?
   Yes = 1 point

5. Do you think that every activity and decision-making process around your church takes twice as long as it should?
   Yes = 1 point

6. Does your congregation blame much of what goes wrong on a lack of money?
   Yes = 5 points

7. Is your worship service more or less exactly the same as it was twenty years ago?
   Yes = 5 points

8. Is there someone in the congregation who seems to grab all the attention no matter what is going on?
   Yes = 10 points

9. Is there constant talk about growth but no actual growth?

   Yes = 5 points

10. Do you wish that the pastor would retire or just leave?

    Yes = 10 points

11. Do you avoid a particular group (choir, prayer team, etc.) because it seems to be a center for gossip?

    Yes = 3 points

12. Do you usually look at your watch during the worship service?

    Yes = 1 point each for the number of times you look at your watch

13. Is there clutter in the church meeting rooms and hallways?

    Yes = 1 point

14. Is there a significant goof in the newsletter or Sunday bulletin most of the time?

    Yes = 1 point

15. Is there an endowment, but hardly any people in attendance on a given Sunday? (e.g., a ratio of endowment to average Sunday attendance that is greater than $100,000 per person could indicate a problem)

    Yes = 5 points

16. Are you now, or will you soon be, in the search process for a new pastor?

    Yes = 10 points

17. Was someone verbally abusive to you or someone else at a recent church event?

    Yes = 10 points + 10 more points if no one did anything about it

18. Has Sunday attendance been declining more or less steadily for at least ten years?

    Yes = 10 points

19. Has there been a major change in the environment of your church (e.g., major business closing or layoffs, natural disaster, trouble in the judicatory or denomination)?

    Yes = 5 points

20. Did the pastor just run off with the organist, church secretary, or acolyte?

    Yes = 10 points + 10 more points if you think the pastor's departure solves your problem

21. Did a member of the staff recently set fire to the church?

    Yes = 20 points

22. Was the treasurer or other church official recently charged with embezzling church funds?

    Yes = 10 points + 10 more points if you think a conviction will solve your problem

23. Is there someone collecting money for a steeple and asking that the checks be made payable to him or her?

    Yes = 10 points

24. Did someone recently circulate during the worship service a petition for the dismissal (or the return) of the pastor?

    Yes = 20 points

25. Does the youth group consist of the pastor's children and their friends who don't go to your church?

    Yes = 5 points

0–5 points. Grab a lily and lie down. The Rapture will be upon you and your congregation soon.

5–10 points. Read the book; it may help you help your congregation.

10–15 points. Read the book; buy several more copies and give them to the lay leaders and/or pastor as needed.

15–20 points. Read the book. Look up the phone number of your judicatory official and write it inside the cover. Call him or her and demand help or the name and number of a good consultant.

20 or more points. Read the book then 1) call a consultant or 2) call 911 and/or 3) name the beast in your midst and wear body armor to church; use the book to prop the door open while people leave.

F.A.Q.s

Interim Ministry and the Search Process

1. *Our pastor who has been with us for 22 years just announced that she will retire in three months. What will happen to us?*

   Good things are likely to happen, especially if the pastorate was a good one. You should use the next three months to celebrate the pastor's ministry with you while lay leaders begin preparations for the interim period. Your judicatory staff is well prepared to assist you through this time and give you the resources you will need to follow your denomination's recommended process.

   If the 22-year pastorate was a series of train wrecks, then the interim time is a good time to figure out why things did not go well and to ensure that the church does not repeat previous errors. This time you will call the right person and you will have a clear picture of where you are called to go.

   Read Chapter 7.

2. *Our pastor just ran off with the organist. Should we call the police or the bishop first?*

   If the pastor took the Sunday offering as well, call the police, then the bishop. Otherwise, just call the bishop. Then fasten your seat belts.

   Read Chapter 7.

3. *Our pastor is about to leave. Can't we just get another pastor right away? Why does the diocese/synod/conference make us do this interim thing?*

   There are several reasons:

   - It takes time to find the right new pastor.
   - The congregation is more likely to find the right pastor when it takes the time to do a self-study.

- The congregation will better bond with a new pastor if it has gotten over the previous pastor, regardless of whether ministry with the previous pastor was a good experience or not.

4. *Why does the interim period have to be so long?*

It takes time to do the three things in the answer to the previous FAQ.

5. *All we need the interim pastor to do is conduct the Sunday services. Why can't we have a part-time interim pastor and save ourselves some money?*

OK. Which things that your departing pastor did regularly do you not want your Interim Pastor to do? Prepare and deliver good sermons? Make hospital visits? Lead weekly Bible Study? Attend board meetings? You get the point.

6. *Why is the interim pastor changing what we do in worship? Doesn't she know we have done worship the same way for years?*

First of all, any clergy person coming to your church is likely to have a liturgical style that is at least slightly different from whatever you have been doing. More importantly, unless your church chooses to remain static, your new settled pastor will be expected to make changes in the worship services depending upon what you say you want, for example, more youth involvement, more contemporary worship, attracting newcomers, etc. A good interim pastor will soften the impact of more substantial changes in worship that may be coming along with the new pastor. When your interim pastor departs, the parish should be better prepared to accept something new.

Conflict

7. *I know something really bad about our church that only a few people know. Should I tell the Conference Minister/Bishop?*

First of all, is the really bad thing a fact or a rumor? Be sure you are dealing only with facts. If you have firsthand knowledge of the big secret, tell the clergy or lay leader as appropriate. If you think it's not appropriate to tell either one, then tell the appropriate person on your judicatory staff. Also, check your goal in sharing the information. Are you trying to achieve justice as you see it or help your church be the best it can be? (Bear in mind that justice is probably not attainable by you or anyone else in this plane of reality.)

See Chapter 6.

8. *This church would be a happy family if a few people just left. Can we make someone leave?*

This is the fantasy of all parish clergy. Really. Don't let them tell you otherwise. Just about every parish has someone who seems to lack good sense or basic social skills and causes problems the pastor and staff must fix regularly. While these people need to be confronted, the confrontation has to be done the right way. If after confrontation the annoying individual chooses to leave, say a prayer of thanksgiving and move on. Also, regarding the "happy family," unless your family escaped en masse from the Home for the Terminally Euphoric, then we'll bet it wasn't happy all the time.

See Chapter 3.

9. *The problem here is poor communication. The rector/pastor and vestry/board don't tell us what is going on. How can we improve our communications?*

We have yet to find a church that was completely satisfied with the quality of their internal communications. Sometimes the problem is that the message that should have been sent sat in someone's mental out-basket and did not actually get distributed. More likely, the message went out but was garbled somewhere along the way. It seems so simple, but it is really hard to be sure everyone in a church knows about and understands everything that goes on.

See Chapter 9.

Strategic Planning

10. *We seem to be OK as a congregation, but we know we are aging and not attracting any young adults. What can we do?*

There really is no short answer to this. You will need to do some serious soul searching. Are you called by God to be the kind of church that will attract young adults in your area? Are you prepared to do what it takes to make that happen? Are you willing to give up something to follow that calling? If the answers are "yes," "yes," and "yes," then see Chapters 2, 3, and 8.

11. *I am weary of having meetings to write a new mission statement. Is it really necessary?*

In this book we suggest creating a statement of purpose rather than a mission statement. There is a difference, and the difference will eliminate the need to rewrite the mission statement every three years or so. Is it "necessary"? Is coherence important?
See Chapter 2.

12. *I am the chairperson for the strategic planning team in our church. We have been holding meetings and circulating a questionnaire to find out what the members envision for the future of the parish. So far all of their suggestions are about improving the quality of the children's choir that consists exclusively of the Pastor's children. How can I get them to think about new ministries?*

First have them reread the description of the early church in Acts 2. Then do whatever you must do to open them to the Holy Spirit. Give them some "right brain" activity to get things started: crayons, clay, poetry, music, etc. If that doesn't work, tell them to go visit churches in the area that are growing. If they don't like those churches because they project the song texts on a screen, then go and find some new members who are interested in the future.

Church Life

13. *I'm tired of being the chairperson for [The Book Sale, The Christmas Pageant, the Fair, The Big Event], but I can't find anyone else who will take this on. Should I just quit?*

Yes. Next question. Seriously, when there is no energy in a church for the Big Event that has been done for years, then it may be time to retire the event for a while or forever. Neither the world nor the parish will come to an end. Let it go. Coke stopped making New Coke when that marketing strategy failed. Know when to cut your losses.

See Chapter 6.

14. *Our Church is over 200 years old and is visited by people who come to see our historic building and stained glass. We are proud of our heritage and work hard to raise the money to keep the building maintained, but it gets harder every year. What can we do?*

You could change your non-profit status from that of church to museum. Then you could seek government and foundation grants to keep the building up and ask the visitors to make "contributions" in exchange for tours. But perhaps you also want to keep on being a church. Well, in that case you may have to decide what you are. It will be hard to be both a church and a museum. You might try the English cathedral solution of putting a café in the crypt.

15. *How come Jesus didn't start any churches?*

- He didn't want to be a Pope.
- The disciples were enough trouble.
- He had the good sense not to.

Messianic preachers who start churches can end up like Jim Jones, serving poison instead of new life in Christ. Jesus kept pointing to God the Creator and promised the presence of God the Spirit. If we asked ourselves in our churches, "What would

Jesus do?" and actually did it, we would most likely sell our real estate and silver communion sets, give the money to the poor, speak out against injustice in our neighborhoods, and recognize Jesus in each other.

See Matthew, Mark, Luke, and John.

–1–

Your Dysfunctional Church

Everything we do, beloved, is for the sake of building you up. For I fear that when I come, I may find you not as I wish, and that you may find me not as you wish; I fear that there may perhaps be quarreling, jealousy, anger, selfishness, slander, gossip, conceit, and disorder.

—2 Corinthians 12:19b–20

People talk about 'dysfunctional' families; I've never seen any other kind.

–Sue Grafton

Thanks to self-help books and TV talk shows, pretty much everyone knows about "dysfunctional families." Church families can be dysfunctional, too. The reality is that all churches, being made up of imperfect human beings, are "dysfunctional" to some degree.

We once served a church that had experienced a string of failed pastorates. While the clergy may have made some errors, the fact that the congregation's troubles had extended through the tenure of several pastors suggested that the problem was not entirely with the clergy. Some parishioners who were concerned about their church's health approached us with the plea: "Please don't tell us that we're a dysfunctional church." It was bad enough to know that they had problems, but apparently the label "dysfunctional" was more than they could bear.

What are we really saying when we use this term? Obviously if something is "functional," it works. "Dys" comes from a Greek root meaning "ill" or "broken." So to call something "dysfunctional" doesn't mean that it doesn't work and never can be right. On the contrary, the implication is that something that is broken or ill can be mended or cured.

However, some dysfunctional churches are flirting with death as they resist all efforts to be mended. For these churches we say, "Turn the lights out when you're done." A bishop told the story of a little old lady who approached him at the coffee hour and said, "Bishop, please don't close this church until after we're all dead and buried." That congregation is ready for hospice care.

One of the reasons churches sometimes choose to remain dysfunctional is that staying sick is easier than getting healthy. A healthy church will be expected to do something really scary: take the Gospel seriously. So your church's dysfunction, whatever it is, may be an avoidance mechanism. By engaging in habitual internal wrangling or constantly whining about not having enough money, a church can avoid getting into actual ministry, which might prove to be risky or uncomfortable. Remarkably, a congregation can sit in church every Sunday and hear the stories about Jesus, then go right on pouring their energy into perpetuating brokenness rather than becoming whole. Wallowing in the pain of the sinful human condition is apparently easier than picking up a cross and seeing what that might lead to.

This chapter catalogues several different kinds of dysfunctional churches. Your church may fit one or more categories. If not, see if you can get your money back on this book.

What Flavor of Dysfunctional Are You?

The "Pastor-is-the-Star" Church

Cardinal Rector. Herr Pastor. It's one thing to have a charismatic leader; however, exclusive dependence on this human person will lead to heartache because *someday this person is going to leave.* It's also possible that this person will make a huge mistake that will leave his (or her) clay feet horribly exposed. Jesus Christ is not available to run our parishes, so if you think your pastor is Jesus, think again.

This church model appears to be declining as churches increasingly move away from being monolithic institutions towards becoming more decentralized relational groups. The increase in the number of female clergy is also gradually reducing the number of churches that seek and empower "stellar" pastors, since this role seems to be more a problem for those with testosterone.

The bottom line here is that empowering the laity is the primary job of clergy, not the other way around.

The Stuck Church

This church prides itself on being able to say, "We always did it this way," and "If it ain't broke, don't fix it." Its motto is, "We owe it to previous generations of church members to, uh, honor the previous generations."

> **Q.** How many Stuckwood Church members does it take to change a light bulb?
>
> **A.** Change it? I'll have you know my grandmother *gave* the church that bulb!

Consistency is the primary virtue for the stuck church, even if it means that they have, like Lot's wife, turned into a fixed pillar. It's an understatement to say that "Stuckites" are content with being who they are. They don't want to change, don't see any need to change, and will resist anyone or anything that tries to make them change. They may think that their "contemporary" worship service is cutting edge, even though they have been doing that service exactly the same way for twenty-five years. The average age of the stuck congregation continues to climb ever higher. Unless something happens to force change upon them, they are heading for the scenario that calls for the last person to leave the building to turn out the lights. Do they trust God or what?

The Delusional Church

This church is also stuck but they don't know it. Call them the Little Church Inside-Your-Head. Their prevailing concept of what the church should be is based upon childhood memories or romantic fantasies of congregational life. The core element of this church's identity is often "We are one big happy family," and may include the corollary delusion "We are friendly and welcoming." They may even have a mission statement and think that they are on a mission (to be friendly?). They also believe that "We have a creed, so we must be theologically coherent." This church might appear to be content to remain small and have a part-time pastor, but it's a trap for the clergy because the fantasy Little Church Inside-Your-Head is famous for its wonderful, self-sacrificing pastor who works tirelessly without regard for compensation and even shovels the snow from the church steps. Any clergyperson who gets caught up between the congregation's fantasy about itself and the reality of limited resources is headed for burnout!

The Addictive Church

This is a particular kind of delusional church in which the members think one of three things: *I go to church to feel good; I go to church to make other members feel good; or I go to church to make the pastor feel good.* A variation is that the pastor thinks that his or her job is to make the congregation feel good. In this church everyone expects the worship service to be a feel-good experience. The sermons all have happy endings. The coffee hour may be genial, but the real juice is in the hushed conversations in the parking lot and lively email exchanges. Everybody is into everybody else's business in the inappropriate way that professionals call "enmeshed" or "fused." Porous boundaries abound. Someone in this dysfunctional system may actually be a sexual or substance abuser.

If it were possible to put an entire parish into a Twelve Step Program, that would be the cure—but only if they are "sick and tired of being sick and tired."

The Pitiful Church

These people have been through a lot and it's not their fault—maybe. The previous pastor died in the pulpit. The one before him was a child molester and arsonist. A tornado ripped off the roof and trashed the organ. Attendance is half what it used to be. There's not enough money to buy hymnals or Christian education materials. The Sunday School superintendent begins her recruiting pitch to prospective teachers by saying, "You probably don't want to do this and don't have time anyway. . . ." Mainline Protestantism has a lot of these struggling churches, and there are more of them every day. Judicatory executives spend a lot of time and energy trying to reinvigorate these churches, but there is a limit to what can be done by hand-holding or infusions of denominational cash.

It's time for this church to put up or shut up. These churches often have resources they have forgotten about—an old parsonage, a piece of land, an endowment, not to mention volunteer time and talents—that can be used in new ways. They should either use these resources or give them to someone who will.

The Poor Church

This variation on the Pitiful Church applies to many of our parishes. This church may not in fact be poor at all, but is always struggling to generate enough money to meet even a minimal budget. Large or small, urban, suburban, or exurban, these churches look for corners to cut: a volunteer to run the website, a member of the church to be the parish secretary or organist for little pay, and, worst of all, deferred maintenance on the church buildings.

In our experience churches that really are poor, even though the members are pledging the best they can, are the ones that are the best stewards of what they have as well as the most generous with their outreach. The story of the Widow's Mite applies to churches. Poverty is not about the bank account but about the human heart.

The Busy Church

The busy church is the medium-to-large church run amok. This church engages in ministry simply by multiplying its activities. Weekly announcements at this church can take forever. The energy in a church like this reminds you of a gymnasium with thousands of college basketball fans shaking the rafters by jumping up and down. There is lots of energy, but it isn't necessarily going anywhere. Members may have plenty of opportunities for Christian formation, outreach, and social events, but when, if ever, do they sit still and pray?

Less chatter and more listening for God's call will give this congregation more focus for their busy-ness, and then they might actually go somewhere.

The "We-Want-to-Grow" Church

Like the Poor Church, there are a lot of these. What does this congregation really want, and more to the point, why do they want it? Do they want to grow so they can have a bigger budget, more staff, more volunteers, a bell choir, or a projection screen system like the church down the street? If you "wannabe" a bigger church, it's important to know *why* you want to grow and to give some thought to what those new people you're looking for will bring to your church. Are they of a different generation, sexual orientation, or racial/ethnic/social background? We understand that we should love the unchurched and their (sometimes ill-behaved) children, but it's easier to love them at a distance. How do we get them to come? How do we get them to stay? Can you say, "We love our neighbors" and mean it?

A sub-type of this church is the **"We-Want-More-Youth" Church**. Older members claim to want more youth but don't want to run the youth program and are reluctant to pay somebody else to do it. Building a successful youth program where none exists means attracting the families of youth to the church and having patience. Youth ministry is about successful relationships. Youth respond well to depth rather than breadth, spirituality rather than functionality, prayer rather than placating.

The Wasteful Church

In all honesty, most churches probably have this problem to some degree. It is easy to talk the talk of Creation Theology, but when it comes to walking the walk in our wasteful consumer society, this church either doesn't know how to be environmentally responsible or is just lazy. The church should audit its buildings and programs for energy efficiency and environmental effects, giving thought to such things as the use of disposable paper cups, parking lots for cars that bring single passengers to church events, and non-renewable energy sources. (The newly revived youth program could be a good resource for getting the audit done.) Our churches must model the environmentally responsible behavior we increasingly expect of everyone. And if there is added cost for being green, it is the cost of an important ministry by example.

The Denominational Church

Some people are diehard Methodists or Episcopalians or Baptists. Churches are always grateful to find these loyal souls. But relying exclusively on denominational loyalty to fill the membership rolls has no future. This is partly the result of the calcification of denominations and partly an evolution of the Body of Christ as a social institution. Denominations have not always existed; Jesus was not a member of your denomination. If a denomination is to reinvent itself (and if this is worth doing), they need to start by checking their own mission statement. What, exactly, is the denomination's reason for being? Congregations need to put their denominational identity in perspective in their particular context and use it—or not—appropriately.

The Conflicted Church

A congregation can get into a snit about most anything. This book has examples of issues large and small that have occupied the time and energy of otherwise smart, sensible people. Sometimes a conflict is actually a reasonable debate about an important decision, such as a discussion about what it will mean to be openly inclusive of gays and lesbians. That's "good conflict." But too much of the time the debate is not so much about an issue as about the merits of the people engaged in the debate. Sometimes one of the parties involved just likes to cause trouble. If you have two or three of these people in your church, you are in for a rough ride. Anonymously send them brochures for churches in neighboring towns.

Fixes and Cures

Most of these dysfunctions will be covered in more depth in following chapters, but meanwhile, here are a few things to keep in mind:

- Don't be afraid. God is in this enterprise with you.
- Know who you are and know what God has in mind for you.
- Do what you must do to be comfortable with change—or be a hermit.
- Work with the resources God has given you—*all of them.*

Going to the Core

As you read the last chapter on the various types of dysfunctional churches, you may have found your church somewhere in that list. Don't panic; you have lots of company. Whether you are the clergy leader, a lay leader, or a person who goes to church no more than once a month, there may be times when you wonder why you bother to go there at all. Yet in spite of the fact that the church is dysfunctional, you worship, pledge, serve on a committee, and do whatever else you do. What do you think is holding you in this church? And what holds the church itself together?

In subsequent chapters we will explore these questions by laying out a methodology for getting down to the core elements of a congregation. If the parish can be compared to a well of water for thirsty souls, we invite you to swim with us to the bottom of the well.

NOTE! These chapters are not like those in the previous book, Ten Dumb Things Churches Do. Rather than naming a "dumb thing" and analyzing it, our approach here will be to dip into congregational development theory. Now that may sound like an opportunity to put this book down and take a nap. That's OK. If you are not feeling up to it today, skip over to the "Nuts and Bolts" section. Clergy and others who want to know the "why" of everything will, we hope, find "Going to the Core" interesting and helpful. The appendix includes an outline for a workshop to help you take members of your church through a study of this material.

—2—

Mission Statements:
Vision, Envision, Revision

*Now I appeal to you, brothers and sisters, by the name of our Lord
Jesus Christ, that all of you should be in agreement and that
there be no divisions among you, but that you should
be united in the same mind and the same purpose.*

—1 Corinthians 1:10

*The place God calls you to is the place where your deep gladness and
the world's deep hunger meet.*

—Frederick Buechner, *Wishful Thinking: A Theological ABC*[2]

The Problem of the Mission Statement

Mission statements are "in." It seems that lately every sort of expert
from personal coaches and organizational consultants to football
coaches and fundraising managers has been promoting the impor-
tance of having a mission statement, that is, a carefully focused set of
words that guides you into the future. Most churches have mission
statements, and any who don't think they *should* have one.

We have long advocated clear mission statements for churches
whenever we have worked with a parish on strategic planning or a
pastoral search. One church following this advice held a two-day
retreat to create a new mission statement. After a lively conversation

about the congregation's values and the scriptural imperatives that were important to them, they came up with something like this:

- St. Swithin's is a welcoming church in the town of East Cupcake that proclaims the Good News of Jesus Christ.

Their mission statement is fine—as far as it goes. Because it is so broad and lacking in specifics, however, it did not do much to help the church's strategic planning committee set priorities for the next three years.

Another church's strategic planning team created a mission statement by using data from the parish survey that had gathered the hopes and desires of the members. At the all-parish meeting where the new draft mission statement was introduced, an argument broke out over whether they really needed a new mission statement. A couple of people who had been involved in writing the previous mission statement were offended. Then it turned out that no one could remember what the former mission statement actually said!

The creation of a brief statement of a church's guiding vision certainly *seems* like a worthwhile endeavor. In our experience of working with churches on mission statements, however, the results have often been disappointing. In fact, all church mission statements seem to be much the same from one congregation to another, regardless of denomination.

Most mission statements go something like this:

We + [verb: present affirmation or future intention] + [descriptor] + [activity]

Examples:

- We are an open and affirming United Church of Christ congregation and we desire to be disciples of Christ in East Cupcake.
- We are a loving, caring community of believers and we strive to welcome all people to join us in worship, Bible study, and outreach.

Such statements may tell an outsider something about the good intentions of the churches that wrote them. But of what practical use are they to the churches?

The following chart, based on this formula, would make it possible to construct a generic mission statement by choosing elements from each column, like ordering dishes from a Chinese menu.

TIME FRAME	WE + VERB	DESCRIPTORS*	ACTIVITIES*
Past to present	We are . . .	historic in the [name of town, neighborhood, etc.] [name of Denomination] loving welcoming open and affirming disciples of Jesus Christ a family a community the Body of Christ believers	Reconciliation Worship Bible study Outreach Christian formation Making disciples
Future	We endeavor to. . . We desire to . . . We strive to. . . We hope to . . .	share the Good News welcome affirm follow Jesus Christ serve those in need	

* Descriptors and Activities can be the things that the church does now, hopes to do in the future, or both.

Perhaps one reason these nonspecific mission statements tend not to be very helpful is that their real purpose is unclear. We think a mission statement is something our church *should* have, but we're not actually sure *why* we should have them. Should a mission statement be a description of the present values of the congregation, an expression of their hope for the future, or both? It is also unclear *for whom* the mission statement is written. Is it for the current congregation, potential members, or perhaps the budget and finance committee? We always look to the budget process as the acid test: Can the budget committee actually be guided by the mission statement?

So while clergy, consultants, and judicatory officers generally agree that a mission statement is a good thing for a congregation to have, unfortunately that is where the agreement ends. Opinions regarding such matters as the content of the mission statement and how often it should be rewritten vary widely. And as we have seen, it is difficult to create a mission statement that is sufficiently specific and future-oriented to describe a genuine calling.

Our solution for the problem of vague and unhelpful mission statements is to take an entirely different approach. We propose discarding the term "mission statement" completely and starting over again.

Core Identity and Envisioned Future

James C. Collins and Jerry I. Porras[3] have defined some useful terms for creating clarity of purpose and mission in a business. They write:

> A well-conceived vision consists of two major components: core ideology and envisioned future. Core ideology, the yin in our scheme, defines what we stand for and why we exist. Yin is unchanging and complements yang, the envisioned future. The envisioned future is what we aspire to become, to achieve, to create—something that will require significant change and progress to attain.[4]

Our proposed alternative approach to the problem of mission and vision statements for churches uses Collins and Porras' distinctions of **core ideology and envisioned future**. Clearly, churches are not the same as businesses. Businesses can begin from many different values, skills, and interests, whereas all Christian congregations spring from the same scriptural roots (even if their understanding of scripture varies widely). So to adapt Collins and Porras' model to churches, we will use instead of "core ideology" the term "**core theology**." We will follow Collins and Porras in subdividing core ideology ("core theology" for us) into "**core values**" and "**core purpose**."

For the church, then, **core theology** (made up of **core values** and **core purpose**) leads to the congregation's **envisioned future**.

CORE THEOLOGY =
CORE VALUES
+
CORE PURPOSE

THE
ENVISIONED
FUTURE

Core Theology

A congregation's core theology is the intangible web of belief that transcends changes of clergy and lay leaders, the societal context, and even transitions from one generation to the next. Core theology may change slightly over time, but only at a glacial pace.

Core theology is comprised of **values** and **purpose**. To illustrate, we will take an example from business. A person considering starting a bookstore might say:

- "I believe that literacy is important for the development and maintenance of a civilized society." (**value**)
- "I desire to sell books at affordable prices in an environment conducive to a discussion about books and ideas." (**purpose**)

In a business it is easy to see that the **purpose** springs naturally from the **values**, but in a church the connection is a little more ambiguous.

For any organization the core ideology, along with the purposes and values that arise from it, comes primarily from the founders. That is clear enough in the case of the emerging bookstore. But what about a congregation's core theology? A church's core theology comes from at least two layers of founders. First, there are the teachings of Jesus and the beliefs of the founders we read about in the New Testament—the disciples, the early church, and Paul. The second layer of theological underpinnings includes documents generated by the founder(s) of a denomination—Luther, Knox, Zwingli, Cranmer, Wesley, et al. It is possible that a third layer of beliefs might be inherited from the founders who started the particular congregation, for example, a group of laypeople, a judicatory leader, or the national mandate of a denomination. In the case of an independent church, the founding pastor (who may still be in the pulpit) would be a guide to the core theology. It is important to note that the second and third layers of founders are *interpreters* of the original founders. The secondary founders may choose particular scripture passages as core values, such as the commandment to make disciples (Matthew 28:19), The Great Commandments (Matthew 22:37), or the practice of snake handling (Mark 16:18). While all of these texts are in the same Bible, obviously they result in a significantly different core theology.

The Book of Common Prayer of the Episcopal Church in the United States includes a catechism that lays out the denomination's core theology about the church (ecclesiology) in the form of questions and answers:

Q. What is the Church?

A. The Church is the community of the New Covenant.

Q. What is the New Covenant?

A. The New Covenant is the relationship with God given by Jesus, the Messiah, to the apostles; and, through them, to all who believe in him.

Q. What is the mission of the Church?

A. The mission of the Church is to restore all people to unity with God and each other in Christ.

Q. How does the Church pursue its mission?

A. The Church pursues its mission as it prays and worships, proclaims the Gospel, and promotes justice, peace, and love.

Q. Through whom does the Church carry out its mission?

A. The Church carries out its mission through the ministry of all its members.[5]

For an Episcopal congregation setting out to write down its core theology, these statements would certainly be a good place to begin. So, for example, working from the Catechism one could write the following core theology for St. Swithins:

- **Core Values:** We are people of the New Covenant who are in relationship with Jesus Christ and all others who believe in Him.

- **Core Purpose:** Our purpose is to restore all people to unity with God and each other in Christ by engaging in prayer and worship, proclaiming the Gospel, and promoting justice, peace and love through the ministry of all of our members.

Note that in this example core theology is broken out into the components of core values and core purpose.

Core Values

The core values for any church will certainly have some basis in scripture. They may also resemble some of the descriptors for mission statements, such as:

- the Body of Christ
- family
- believers
- historic
- welcoming
- open and affirming
- disciples

"The Body of Christ" is a scripturally sound descriptor of Christian community anywhere, any time. Paul uses it again and again in his letters to churches: "So we, who are many, are one body in Christ" (Romans 12:5), or "We are one in Christ" (Galatians 3:28). So it is probably safe to say as part of a core values statement that St. Swithin's is "the Body of Christ."

However, if we state that St. Swithin's is a "family," that opens a can of worms. For what do we mean by "family"? A "traditional" nuclear family with a mother and father and two children, a blended family of a mother and father in second marriages, a single mother with her children, or a same-sex couple with or without children?

"Historic" is another heavily freighted, non-scriptural word that turns up in church mission statements. The congregation may indeed be hundreds of years old, but is that a *value* or simply a *fact*? If it is a fact that controls the congregation's decision-making, then it is also a *value*. A question for such a congregation is: How does this value rank relative to being the Body of Christ?

A 250-year-old congregation had owned a rectory next to the church for more than a hundred years. The house had originally been built in the late eighteenth century by one of the town's leading citizens. In the face of the contemporary trend for clergy desiring to build equity in their own homes rather than living in church-owned housing, the church contemplated selling the rectory.

Many members argued that the rectory should be retained because of its "historical value." Clearly for the members of this congregation, owning "historical" real estate was itself a core value. "Historical value" is a tricky business for many churches. They must grapple with such questions as whether the preservation of stained glass windows is more or less important than repairing the organ or sustaining the soup kitchen.

Peeling back the layers of a congregation's principles to find its core values may uncover genuine, scripturally based values that any church would be proud to claim. On the other hand, that exercise may lead to the discovery that the congregation is in reality a chapel for one prominent family or a club for many families. The problem of claiming one set of beliefs while acting according to completely different beliefs will be covered later. For now, we will assume a solid set of scripturally based core values that resemble the values of most Christian congregations.

Core Purpose

The core purpose is the church's reason for being. We might expect this to be more idealistic than the purpose of a for-profit business. Let's look again at the core value and purpose of the bookstore:

- "I believe that literacy is important for the development and maintenance of a civilized society." (**value**)
- "I desire to sell books at affordable prices in an environment conducive to a discussion about books and ideas." (**purpose**)

As we have seen, the would-be bookseller's purpose springs naturally from the value. However, the value that "literacy is important for the development and maintenance of a civilized society" could give rise to different purposes. Our bookseller's core value could result in a core purpose of establishing a bookstore or a library or a school. Similarly, the fact that your church believes in Jesus Christ (i.e., your core value) may translate into preaching or serving or praying, differing purposes that could in turn lead you to stand on a street corner and preach, start a homeless shelter, or become a contemplative hermit.

Any of these activities could be covered by the examples of core value and core purpose offered above for St. Swithin's. The core purpose for the congregation should be specific enough to differentiate the church community from a monastery on one hand and a country club on the other:

- The core purpose of St. Swithin's is to be a *Christian congregation* endeavoring to restore all people to unity with God and each other in Christ.

A church's context is important in defining its core purpose. An urban church will likely see its purpose as different from that of a suburban or rural church. A small town church may have a particular role to play in the community that should be stated as a core purpose.

- The core purpose of St. Swithin's is to be a Christian community *in the village of East Cupcake*, endeavoring to restore all people to unity with God and each other in Christ.

Regardless of the church's core purpose, its purpose statement should be permitted to change as the context changes. When, for example, the neighborhood demographic alters or a previously thriving town faces long-term economic hardship, the purpose statement may need adjustment.

- The core purpose of St. Swithins is to be a Christian community in the village of East Cupcake, endeavoring to restore all people to unity with God and each other in Christ, *especially by serving the poor and the homeless in our midst.*

Or, if the core purpose is "to make disciples," the congregation needs to decide whether they can best do that by preaching the Gospel, enacting the Gospel, or doing both. Looking at the specifics of the context is a good place to start. For example, given the core purpose of making disciples, can the congregation locate many unchurched people in their area whom they can persuade to visit their church, or would they be better off sending a mission team to the nearest large city or perhaps overseas? There are many modes of evangelism available to a congregation. The belief that the church exists "to make disciples" should motivate the members to seek the most fertile mission field open to them and to utilize the gifts they have. Both the mission field and the gifts of the members will change over time, while the core purpose will not.

Writing Down Your Core Values and Core Purpose

Here is a pair of templates you can use to help your church write down its **core values** and **core purpose**:

CORE VALUE STATEMENT: WHO WE ARE

We + verb	Value (or belief) that defines us
We are...	...the Body of Christ ...a Christian family ...making disciples ...living the Good News
We believe...	...that Jesus Christ is Lord ...that God is reconciling all people ...in the priesthood of all believers ...in the Great Commandments (love God and love neighbor as self)

CORE PURPOSE STATEMENT: OUR REASON FOR BEING

We + [optional verb implying intent] +	To + [verb]	+ Object
We desire intend endeavor strive	worship praise glorify obey serve honor heal love	God Jesus Christ the Holy Spirit all people neighbors the people of our town, city, etc. the poor, the prisoner, the oppressed, etc.

If you look at the mission statement of your own church, can you see a resemblance to these two templates? Can you differentiate between core values and core purpose in your mission statement? Or do your core purposes and values intermingle in a single statement?

Also note the optional "verb implying intent." By including such a verb in your purpose statement, your congregation acknowledges that the Kingdom of God is not yet complete. Without it you have this, for example:

- We glorify God in all that we do and serve Him by serving others . . . etc.

If this statement happens to be true, then you can have a front row seat for the Second Coming. Since it most likely is not, we recommend a more humble statement of *future intent*:

- We **desire** to glorify God in all that we do.

Transmitting Core Theology

Churches subtly convey information about their beliefs in everything they do, from how the service sheet is printed to what is taught in Christian formation classes. Many churches are deliberate about teaching their core theology through an inquirer's class or newcomer's class. Such teaching is part of an informal matching process that helps to sort out those who will fit into the community from those who will not. Since few seekers arrive at the door of the church without beliefs of their own, this process helps new people figure out whether the congregation is their sort of people (and vice versa).

We in the mainline church like to think that we welcome everyone; however, the fact is that people who do not share a parish's core theology will be at odds with the organization. For example, a church with a progressive attitude about inclusiveness will have a difficult time with more conservative folk who want to exclude those they think are "not Christian." People on opposite ends of a values spectrum *can* coexist, but they can also make each other miserable. Unfortunately, our mainline denominations abound with churches split by disagreement over how literally scripture is to be interpreted. Increasingly, churches are inserting certain key words into their core theology statements to signal their position on the liberal-conservative spectrum of scripture interpretation. Words and phrases such as "Bible-centered," "Christ-centered," and "traditional" on one hand, and "inclusive," progressive," and "open and affirming" on the other signal to those who know the code where a congregation stands on a whole package of issues. While there are those who enjoy debating hot-button issues from sunup to sundown, most people want neither to engage in endless dispute about their theology nor to be made to feel uncomfortable about their beliefs. People usually seek churches with core theology that matches their own.

Of course, a congregation's expression of its core theology is of concern in more areas of parish life than how it embraces newcomers. Clergy and lay leaders constantly reinforce core theology through worship, preaching, Bible study, and Christian formation for young and old. Our media-aware age has motivated many churches to vet their print and electronic media to ensure consistency that logos, tags, graphics, and even type font choices consistently reinforce the core theology. One church may carefully emphasize its denominational logo while another deliberately ignores denominational "branding" in favor of a graphic design of its own. A congregation may choose a picture of their historic church building as their key image while another uses a cross. Each image sends a signal about core values.

Discovering Core Theology

By now it should be clear that core theology is not something a congregation can dream up on a weekend retreat. Core theology is a very real thing that can be discerned and reclaimed. However, the discovery process may be complicated because we often have trouble differentiating between what we *actually* believe and what the church says we *should* believe. For example, just about every Christian church hangs its hat on the statement "Jesus Christ is Lord (or Sovereign)." But what individual members may in fact believe is something more along the lines of the Doobie Brothers' song "Jesus Is Just Alright With Me." Church members are notably reticent to articulate what they actually do believe, particularly if their beliefs differ from official church doctrine.

Identifying a church's core theology is challenging, then, because there are layers of belief, and the layers don't necessarily match up. There are the beliefs the institution affirms and the beliefs actually held by individual members. To make matters even more complicated, there is a third layer of beliefs: operational beliefs, or what is commonly referred to in the business world as "corporate culture." Corporate culture may not align with the core theology. For example, if "Jesus is Lord" is the *institutional* belief statement and "Jesus is just alright with me" is the *actual* belief of the members, the congregation may in fact *operate* with the attitude that if Jesus came along, he would not be allowed to be a member because he would cause too much trouble by challenging their materialism, racism, and humanism. The operational belief is that *discipleship is too much trouble.*

Consultants Ruth Wright and Rod Reinecke have developed a tool for sorting and analyzing an organization's actual beliefs, stated beliefs, and operational beliefs. This instrument, which includes a diagnostic test, offers a congregation the ability to discuss analytically how these three layers of beliefs interact.[6]

Here is a picture of how the three layers of core theology might line up:

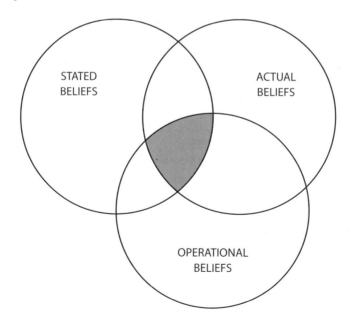

STATED
BELIEFS

ACTUAL
BELIEFS

OPERATIONAL
BELIEFS

The overlapping area allows us to see that only *some* beliefs are actually part of all three layers of core theology. A belief that "worship is an integral part of the Christian life" might be congruent in a church's stated, actual, and operational beliefs, for example. But in the same congregation, such theological concepts as who Jesus is, the role of the Holy Spirit, and the Virgin Birth may well diverge considerably in the three areas.

Ideally there is no discrepancy between an organization's stated, actual, and operational beliefs. However, it may be that complete congruence of core ideology is possible only for the individual entrepreneur working alone or for a congregation of one.

The Envisioned Future

The future calls. Whether your congregation calls the process of discerning the future "long-range planning," "strategic planning," or just "visioning," the idea is the same: determining where God is calling this congregation to go.

In *Ten Dumb Things Churches Do*, Philip suggested three possible sources for ideas for the future:

1. **The parish itself**: its historical trajectory and its present gifts and strengths
2. **Current and projected trends in the context**: neighborhood, region, judicatory, denomination
3. **The Holy Spirit**: any ideas—including wild and crazy ideas— the Spirit might drop on a congregation

Congregations and strategic planning committees should use all three of these sources in discerning God's call into the future. A picture of this process looks something like the one on the next page.

Recently while using this process with a church, we observed that the strategic planning team and the congregation as a whole had no difficulty investigating and analyzing the church's history and strengths and the contextual factors. The part that seemed to be difficult for everyone was finding the wild and crazy ideas that come by way of the Holy Spirit.

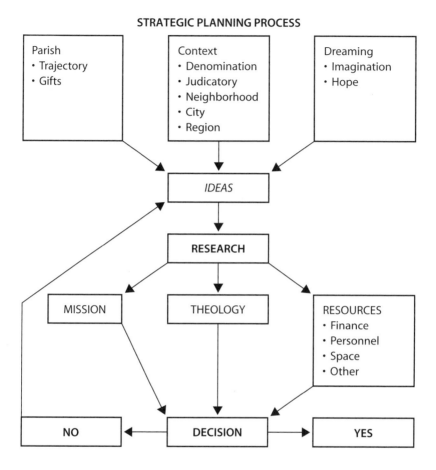

STRATEGIC PLANNING PROCESS

We tried to unlock the door of imagination by asking the same question in different ways:

- Where is the energy?
- Where is the passion?
- Who are the risk-takers and prophets?
- What do they envision?

But no clear responses to these questions were forthcoming. The result for this congregation was a strategic plan focused on fixing perceived problems rather than proposing a bold future. While fixing

problems is a worthy venture, the transforming contribution of the
Holy Spirit seemed to be lacking.

What the strategic planning team produced looked something
like this:

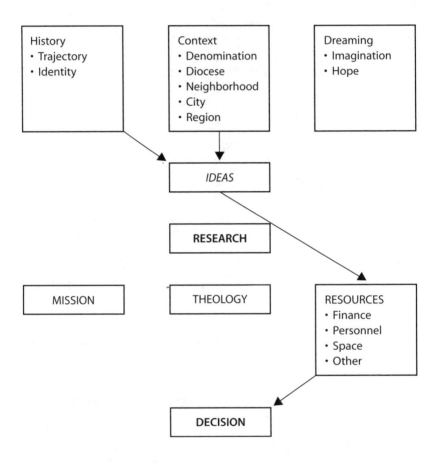

It would be unfair to say that they shut out the Holy Spirit.
Nevertheless, the team was not able to discern any bold calling, and
the action items in the final plan were devoid of any big, daring ideas
for the future.

So What's "The Big Idea"?

We have learned by observing congregations struggle with strategic planning that most have a tendency to stick to analyzing data about their people and their environment. A strategic plan emphasizing data analysis is really more of a market study—not necessarily a bad thing, but not one that produces much discernment of a calling, as the last example showed. It may be that our culture encourages us to develop the more "left brain" functions of analytical thinking and problem solving, while the action of the Holy Spirit is more akin to "right brain" activity involving imagination and creativity. If it is a cultural bias, it is one for which we need to compensate when we engage in visioning exercises.

How can we make the Holy Spirit a more integral part of our planning? Let's return to the three sources outlined above.

First of all, drawing on the church's history is all well and good, so long as one looks at the continuous *flow* of history to the present and the future. If the church has a strong history of outreach in the community and still has energy for it, then it makes sense to include a vigorous outreach program in the future plan.

Second, the same holds true for context. The church should be looking at trends in its neighborhood because God's call will be in the future projections. If, for instance, demographic trends show a steady increase in the population of a particular ethnic group living near the church, then it makes sense for the church to consider a ministry intended for this group.

Third, the congregation should ask some basic questions:

- What is needed in the community, locally or globally?
- What can *we* do?
- What can we do *with help*?
- What is there to do that we have no idea how to do, yet feel called to do?

Looking at trends of history and context may suggest a huge future goal such as the construction of a school or medical facility.

It is also possible for individuals to contribute inspirations that have nothing to do with trends but a lot to do with the congregation's core value and core purpose. For example, a church could decide that they want to be *the* place to go in the neighborhood (or city or state) for spiritual growth, or the study of religion and science, or reconciliation among races. To get the creative visioning juices flowing, it is easier and better to put the historical and contextual trends aside and go back to the core theology and brainstorm some Big Ideas.

Here's a diagram of a strategic planning process that incorporates work on core theology and then discern the "Big Idea":

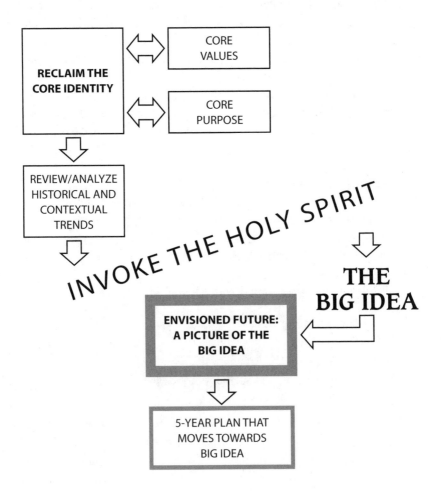

Core values generate a core purpose. A congregation could stop right there and simply carry out the basic purposes intrinsic to their core theology—e.g., worship, Christian formation, and outreach. Since doing even this much well is challenging enough for many congregations, we suggest that parishes work on attaining coherence at this level before tackling the "Big Idea." A church that does not attain congruence of its core theology and core values with what it actually does (core purpose) is likely to go way off base in discerning a Big Idea. We'll say more about the problems of this lack of alignment in the next chapter. The parish that does have coherently stated and operating core theology, however, is ready to engage in discerning a Big Idea that could animate the parish for many years.

Some examples of a Big Idea:

- Establish a hospice facility in the neighborhood
- Start three mission churches in the next twelve years
- Develop a program to send medical missionaries to multiple locations over the next fifteen years
- Begin a school for lay theological training

How big should the Big Idea be? We've seen small churches do amazing things because they were genuinely called by God to do them. If we think that ministry means we do stuff because God wants us to, then we have missed the point. But if part of our core theology is that God is reconciling the world, our role is to *help*, not to *take over*. So, how big should the Big Idea be? The answer is, "As big as your Spirit-inspired imagination."

The Word Made Flesh

Christians are people of the Incarnation; we believe that Jesus Christ, the Word, became flesh and blood by the Holy Spirit. This is also true for the Big Idea. Once we have the Spirit-given idea, we work with the Creator to bring it into being. Envisioning the possibility of the not-yet is an essential part of bringing a Big Idea into being. What would it look like if the church were a regional spiritual center? Perhaps there would be space for retreats, an appropriate library, a staff person dedicated to the spiritual center, etc. What would the church look like if it were a center for racial reconciliation? There might be multi-cultural arts events, a racially or culturally integrated day school, or an endowed institute with a resident scholar. Drawing a literal or verbal picture of the Big Idea invites the Holy Spirit to enter into the future of the congregation.

The Big Obstacle to the Big Idea

It is obvious that if you decide to walk north, you are not going south. No matter what your congregation chooses to do, given finite time and resources, there is always something that you are choosing *not* to do. This simple truth weighs heavily on congregations as they think about the future. A church usually recognizes that if it chooses to do something new, it will need to give up something it is currently doing, unless there is an increase in resources of time or money. And churches are notoriously slow to stop doing anything.

What often happens is that the semi-brave congregation steps out into the future while still clinging to where they are. But that is like stretching one end of a rubber band while the other end remains stuck to a post. If the congregation cannot let go of whatever they are clinging to, the tension becomes unbearable. A common example of something the church can't bear to let go of is the Sunday eight a.m. traditional-style worship service. In many churches, the 8:00 service is attended mostly by a handful of people over the age of sixty-five. There are exceptions to this pattern, but for many congregations the question hovers in the air: "How long do we keep doing this service for a dwindling number of people?"

Perhaps we should remember that not only are we people of the Incarnation, we are people of the Resurrection. The example of Jesus Christ shows us that "life leads to death leads to new life." A program we have done for a while that no longer works may be a sign that we can do something *new*, not a sign that we must continue to operate the program on life support. God is always calling us to use our God-given gifts to join in that great paradigm of new life: "I am about to do a new thing; now it springs forth, do you not perceive it?" (Isaiah 43:19).

Big Idea or . . . ?

Discerning a call is a humbling experience. Unless we can put our egos aside and humble ourselves before God, we are not likely to hear God's voice. This is part of what Jesus meant when he said that we have to lose our lives in order to find them. Of course, discernment is not always only a matter of listening for God. God's energy communicates with us in many ways, so we need to be prepared to use all of our senses. Calling comes out of that Divine Energy. The energy may be in a single leader's voice or in a growing awareness shared by many people. The Holy Spirit may push from behind, walk next to you, or call from a distance ahead. What do the leaders and followers in your church get excited about? Pay attention! It may be the Holy Spirit dropping a Big Idea on you.

❖❖**3**❖❖

Corporate Culture:
Thinking About the Pattern on the Wallpaper

You will know them by their fruits.
—Matthew 7:16

W e want to share with you a hard lesson we learned about the power of corporate culture. Here's the story in Philip's words:

A few years ago I took a break from church consulting to help some friends with the operation of a small hotel with a bar, restaurant, and banquet business. I'll call it the Nowunz Inn. The hotel, located in a small former mining town, was more than 150 years old. Since the decline of the local mining industry, the area's history and "old-timey" atmosphere had made the town a popular tourist destination.

The sellers of the Nowunz Inn provided the buyer, with financial statements that showed the operation to be breaking even. I helped the new owners write a business plan focused on the goal of elevating the hotel from three-star to four-star status. The demographics of the town and surrounding area suggested that with careful attention to marketing and upgrading the service in all departments, it would be possible to steadily raise both the prices and the overall quality of the hotel.

There was, however, a major flaw in the business plan. No one, including me, detected the presence of an invisible but powerful force: a corporate culture that did not support the kind of changes necessary to bring the hotel to four-star status. I supposed—incorrectly, as it turned out—that the employees, when presented with the opportunity to improve the quality of service and subsequently their paychecks, would hop on board the program. In fact, the employees, especially those that had been on the staff for many years, resisted all change efforts mightily.

It seems that our friends were the third set of owners in fifteen years. It turned out that none of the previous owners had made any money. The truth was that the corporate culture was not primarily *about* making money; it was about preserving the hotel as an anchor institution for the small town. This historic hotel was a community symbol that stood for important community values, much the same way certain historic churches function in some old New England towns. Everyone who lives in such a town thinks of the old, white-steepled church as *their* church, whether they ever darken the door or not. Local residents fondly cite family events such as weddings and funerals and baptisms that took place there. Major events in the life of the town, such as concerts and meetings, take place in the church. Some folks feel entitled to ownership by birthright because someone in their family helped build part of the church, and so on.

The Nowunz Inn was much the same kind of symbolic institution. Just about everyone in town was either a former employee or felt connected to the hotel through some past event like a wedding reception, honeymoon, weekly Rotary Club meeting—or else they just hung out in the bar. The historic bar where deals had been struck for 150 years was the place to be and be seen in town. In short, the hotel occupied a central and unchangeable place in the corporate culture of the town. And the key corporate value was preserving the hotel with its bar and restaurant *as it was* for the town, not making it a commercial success.

I joked early on that if I moved a barstool, someone on the other side of town would have a seizure. But as it turned out, it was no joke. The bar regulars told me in my first week not to change anything in the bar. They recounted how one new owner had brought in a fancier model of barstools, with the result that all of the bar regulars took their business elsewhere until the old stools were reinstated. I got the message about the need for stability from the point of view of the local patrons. Unhappily, I did not get it about keeping the corporate culture intact for the employees. To make a long story short, they staged a coup and got rid of me.

What exactly was the corporate culture that I was disturbing? It was the culture of the small town where everyone knows everyone and more value is placed on friendliness than on professional excellence. Outsiders are permitted to come into this culture under the condition that they join the culture, not try to change it. Of course any business plan must answer the question of who its customers are, but were the customers of the Nowunz Inn the laidback townspeople or the sophisticated tourists who visited the area? The corporate culture of the hotel and the town were of one mind on this point: the hotel exists primarily for the townspeople, and if some money can be made from the tourists, that's OK, but it remains a secondary goal.

Ironically, my experience of working within the corporate cultures of numerous churches did not save me from being tripped by the pitfalls of this small-town business, which was operating in much the same way as a church. Ouch!

The lesson in this story for those of us contemplating the corporate culture of our churches is that *the values expressed through a church's corporate culture drive its decision-making.*

A church's corporate culture is manifested in many ways, and we will look at some of them in this chapter. First, however, let's consider *why* the corporate culture is important.

The Significance of Corporate Culture

Corporate culture—the atmosphere in which a congregation lives and breathes and has its being—is important because it embodies the operational beliefs of the community. That atmosphere may be life-giving or it may be toxic.

Looking at the corporate cultures of churches is particularly important at this point in history because recent major changes in secular society have so strongly impacted those corporate cultures.[7] Forty or so years ago the baby boom generation began to rebel against the prevailing institutional values, including the idea that one went to church out of a sense of obligation. We can no longer rely on anyone's sense of obligation to attend church to fill our pews. The simple fact is that more and more we must motivate people to come to our churches, and we must motivate them to stay. Advances in communications technology have also brought about immense cultural changes. New technologies have given us amazing tools with the potential to make everyone a filmmaker, everyone a publisher, everyone a pundit. We swim in a sea of manifold ideas and opinions, in a society in which there is no longer anything approaching a broadly shared social contract or a unanimously agreed upon set of values.

Such major transformations in our society have contributed to the widely lamented decline in church membership in the mainline Protestant denominations. Through these last few decades, as church attendance in mainline churches has steadily eroded, every denomination has put together program after program to attract new members. Some efforts have been successful, while others have been as futile as trying to stop the tide from going out. As an example, during the Episcopal Church's self-proclaimed Decade of Evangelism in the 1990s, church membership actually dropped.

It isn't that churches have ignored change or have refused to try new things. The problem is that they are going about it in the wrong way. Structural and technical changes have fallen short because they are not enough. What is needed is systemic change. Addressing the situation of the church in the new millennium, Anthony B. Robinson writing in *Transforming Congregational Culture* calls for fundamental changes in the corporate culture:

> "Membership decline," while real, did not begin to adequately name our situation. It was and is, an enormous adaptive challenge posed by a newly post-Christendom, post-establishment, post-modern era. . . . For all the mainline Protestant denominations that had once been the religious establishment of a more or less Christian America, where there was a high degree of consensus and homogeneity, the challenge was enormous and painful. It felt like loss and in many ways it was. There was loss of numbers, loss of clout, loss of role, loss of certainty. All this loss, and its attendant grief, has spawned an era of conflict and uncertainty in mainline congregations and denominations. . . . But I honestly believe that these are birth pangs, not death throes.[8]

The reason many earnest efforts to reverse the ebbing tide of church membership failed or fell short was that they focused on structural and programmatic changes in our churches. We did our best to bring in newcomers by blanketing new housing developments with doorknob flyers and placed ads on cable television. We added more services with different kinds of music, offered classes in Christian art, and started book groups.

To motivate people to come *and* to stay, however, we need to be able to articulate who and what we are so the newcomers can say, "Yes, this is what I have been looking for." That includes being able to artic-ulate our corporate culture—the one thing we did *not* change while we were restructuring and adding more niches to our congregational life.

Getting a Handle on Corporate Culture

The label "corporate culture" has gained currency in the business world as a handy way to talk about sets of intangible behaviors and expectations that distinguish one organization from another. It's also useful for characterizing other aspects of our lives, for each of us actu-ally lives daily in overlapping corporate cultures, each with its set of unspoken rules and values. For example, every workplace has a cor-porate culture that includes such things as what you are expected to wear and how long you are allowed to take for lunch. Seasoned trav-elers recognize that train passengers engage a corporate culture that is different from that of bus, airplane, and cruise ship passengers, and so on. Most of us move in and out of these cultures with relative ease, learning the life skill of sizing up a new culture's often unspoken and invisible rules and behavioral norms.

Families exemplify the countless variations that exist in corporate cultures. Each family has its own way of doing things, myriad spoken and unspoken rules and customs that govern such things as the assigning of chores, when and how meals are eaten, which topics are considered suitable for discussion, and what to do at Christmas and other major holidays. When you get married you quickly discover that your spouse's family has a different corporate culture than yours. Do they open the Christmas presents on Christmas Eve, Christmas Day (before or after breakfast), or on Epiphany? God help the newlywed who discovers these important cultural differences by stumbling over them blindly!

Of course, corporate cultures you have lived in for a long time are not something you think about. Try thinking about your own family and how you would describe its corporate culture. Close to impossible, isn't it? It's like asking you to describe the pattern on the wallpaper in your childhood bedroom. Who pays attention to it? It's just *there*!

It's similar with a church's corporate culture. Could you describe it? Probably not, unless you have recently spent time in another church that was somewhat different. A church's corporate culture includes how visitors are greeted (or ignored), the style of worship (formal or informal), the understanding of ministry as inward directed or outward directed toward the community, how decisions are made, who's in charge, and a host of subtle unwritten cues and codes.

In the previous chapter, we used this chart to describe the difference between stated beliefs, actual beliefs, and operational beliefs.

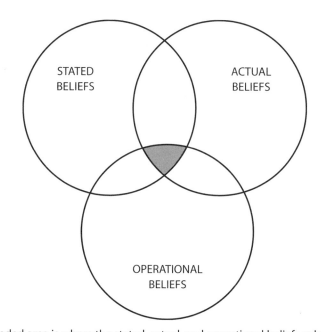

The shaded area is where the stated, actual, and operational beliefs cohere.

We suggested that operational beliefs—that is, the beliefs that govern how the church actually makes decisions—are a key part of the corporate culture. These working values and beliefs that drive decisions will be known by every active member *whether they are written down or not.* Every employee of the Nowunz Inn and every citizen of the town knew the operational beliefs that had governed decision-making.

If operational beliefs and stated beliefs are sufficiently divergent, the congregation becomes just one more institution that says one thing and does another. Obviously, it is confusing to a newcomer to hear from the pulpit that we must love one another when, in fact, it is clear that various groups and individuals in the congregation do *not* love each other. In church conflict consulting, we have often heard the statement, "I thought we were supposed to be a *Christian* congregation, but we sure don't behave like it." This kind of dissonance drives people out of the church, which is certainly one good reason to know what your congregation's corporate culture is.

In the previous chapter we noted that the core values and core purpose are a part of the corporate culture of a congregation. These foundational elements are reinforced in the teaching, preaching, worship life, newsletter, and every other communications medium of the parish. But what about the actual beliefs of the individuals in the organization? How do their beliefs relate to the culture? If the *stated* core values and *operational* core values are not the same, there will be trouble. One of two situations is likely to exist (see next page).

In both examples, espousing one set of beliefs while acting on a different set of beliefs creates tension and expends energy that could be better put to use in doing the ministry.

By contrast, a congregation that has perfect or near-perfect alignment of its stated, actual, and operational beliefs would be a ball of fire. Consider this description of the early church:

> Awe came upon everyone, because many wonders and signs were being done by the apostles. All who believed were together and had all things in common; they would sell their possessions and goods and distribute the proceeds to all, as any had need. Day by day, as they spent much time together in the temple, they broke bread at

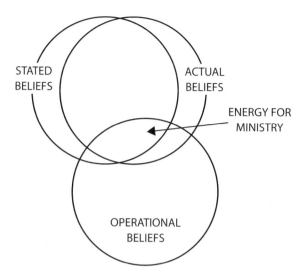

In this congregation the stated beliefs of the organization and the actual beliefs of the members are very similar, but the operational beliefs are different. The sermons may match well with the people's beliefs, but the work of the church proceeds along different lines.

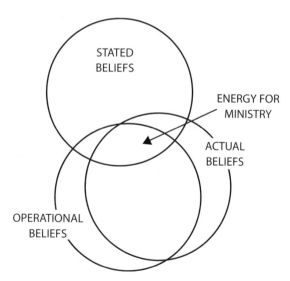

In this congregation the actual beliefs and operational beliefs are similar, but the stated beliefs are different. This may be a smooth-running parish, but no one takes the stated beliefs seriously.

home and ate their food with glad and generous hearts, praising God and having the goodwill of all the people. And day by day the Lord added to their number those who were being saved. (Acts 2:43–47)

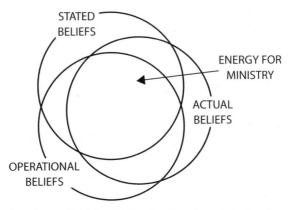

The greater the alignment of beliefs, the less tension there is in the church and the more energy there is for the ministry.

Additional Components of Corporate Culture

Certain manifestations of corporate culture in a church may be obvious, while others may be hard to see. Here are some components of corporate culture that can be found in most churches, along with questions to help you identify them:

- **Spirituality**: Do all meetings start with prayer and/or Bible study? Is there an emphasis on spiritual growth groups, retreats, silence in worship? (The absence of such activities may indicate that the corporate culture does not support public displays of spirituality.)
- **Ministry**: Is the ministry primarily directed inward toward the needs of the congregation or outward toward the community and the world? Is the ministry conventional or innovative? Does the corporate culture allow for new ventures with permission to fail and try again, or not?
- **Authority**: Who's in charge: the pastor, the matriarch/patriarch, vestry, session, God, no one?

- **Management Style**: Do the members of the congregation want to be leaders, co-leaders, collaborators, or followers?
- **Decision-making**: Are there visible pathways for decision-making or are decisions reached by some underground process?
- **Growth**: Does the congregation want to grow in numbers? If so, why? Do they want more volunteers, more families with children, more pledge units? Does the church see growth as a scriptural imperative or an economic necessity?
- **Fellowship**: Is fellowship an activity that supports the ministry or is fellowship the ministry?
- **Money**: Should the pastor talk about it or talk around it? Is the stewardship campaign intended to fill in a budget or is it directly connected to spirituality and ministry?
- **Trust**: Do people trust the clergy? Do the clergy trust the people? Do the people trust each other? Does anyone trust God?
- **The Big Event**: Is there a big annual event that plays a major role in defining the work of the parish all year: The Fair, The Concert, The Book Sale, The Talent Show, etc.?

All of these areas of church life are surrounded by expectations that indicate the church's corporate culture. If the corporate culture truly reflects the core identity of the church and the people are satisfied that their core beliefs are in synch with the Holy Spirit, then all is well. If not, there is the difficult task of making a change.

Discovering Your Church's Corporate Culture

Asking a congregation to define its corporate culture is the equivalent of asking a fish to describe the water it swims in. Yet there is a fairly simple way to begin to uncover the corporate culture your church lives in. All you need to do is take any church activity and ask "why" questions about it. Try the Sunday worship schedule, for example.

Q. Why do you have services at 8 am and 10 am?

A. Because that opens up the hour from 9 to 10 am for adults' and children's Sunday School for people who attend either service.

Q. Why is that important?

A. Because if we did not do this, the members of the two congregations might pass each other in the hallways but never get to know each other.

Q. Why is *that* important?

A. Here are three different responses representing different values:

1. Because we are trying to be the Body of Christ and we recognize that each member is important. (A good theological response reflecting scripturally centered core values. This church honors building up the body of Christ through Christian formation for its children and interactive ministry for the adults.)
2. We are all friends here (i.e., we are a family) and we want to see and be with each other. (This church honors traditional values of family extended to the whole parish.)
3. We always did it this way. (This church honors its past so much they have laminated it and placed it in the middle of the church.)

You get the idea. Asking "why" questions about any activity in your church helps you to begin to extract the operational beliefs—the core values and purpose—that really drive the institution. Do the answers match up with your stated beliefs, or are you uncovering some significantly different operational beliefs?

Somewhere in the atmosphere of corporate culture will be some vitalizing substances such as baptismal vows or the credal and confessional documents of the denomination or possibly some bits of scripture. On the other hand, corporate culture also frequently includes norms of behavior and matters of local interest such as maintaining an historic church with historical buildings, elements that may not be so invigorating.

Another way to discover the corporate culture of your church is to ask the newcomers. Because they haven't yet fully assimilated to your corporate culture, they are likely able to see it more clearly than old-timers. And be prepared to be surprised by what they have to say.

Making Changes in the Corporate Culture

If corporate culture is difficult to uncover, changing it is even more difficult. Therefore, one must be clear whether or not it really *needs* to be changed. How can you tell?

A healthy congregation has a healthy corporate culture. A healthy corporate culture results in most of the members feeling nourished by the church and its activities. Even if a congregation has trouble identifying its corporate culture, members should be able to answer this key question: *How are you being fed by this church?* To put it another way, *Why do you go to this church?* Worship is almost always the number one response, but what comes next? Is it fellowship? Music? Mission trips? Or try this question: *What do you expect to receive from your church?* Love from the members and/or the pastor? Opportunities to join in ministry by serving on committees, singing in the choir, helping in the homeless shelter? Every member has an expectation of how the church will feed him or her. If a significant number of people have the same expectation and the expectation is being met, you have found a part of the corporate culture.

Parish surveys taken during a congregation's search process routinely show some measure of self-satisfaction with the collective expectations *unless* the church has been through some major trauma and turmoil. If people's expectations are being met, there is usually no perceived need to question how or why that is happening.

Because the church is a voluntary organization, members self-select to join based in part on being comfortable with the prevailing corporate culture. You may or may not be conscious of your motivations, but at some level the decision to join a particular church has to do with how well your expectations match up with what is offered by that congregation.

When our churches welcome newcomers, orientation often includes bits of our corporate culture as we talk about our activities and how to become involved, as well as expectations about pledging (usually severely understated lest newcomers be frightened off). However, unlike businesses that impart their corporate culture to new hires through employee training and videos, we do not talk much about policies, procedures, accountability, authority, and the rule of "we always did it this way."

In brief, the health of a church is largely a function of how well members' expectations line up with the corporate culture. If the fit is good, people feel well nourished and institutional health can be assessed by such measures as vigorous ministries and sound steward-ship. A healthy church has a corporate culture that works.

On the other hand, if your church is stuck—i.e., not growing, experiencing aging membership, receiving fewer pledges, etc.—then *something* must surely change or the church will die. Many congrega-tions in this situation—which includes most congregations today— think they can solve their problems simply by working harder at doing the same things they have always done. For a stuck church, however, doing the same old thing merely reinforces the corporate culture *at the very point that the culture needs to be called into question.* If serious problems exist in the parish, then it is possible that the cor-porate culture itself is feeding those problems.

It is easy to overlook the fact that the Gospel is actually an irri-tant to most congregations. The radical nature of Jesus' ministry and teaching is hard for affluent Americans to embrace. Consequently, many churches build into their corporate culture some avoidance mechanism that distracts them from paying too much attention to scriptural imperatives such as "love your enemy."

In one church we worked with, the avoidance mechanism was conflict. These people loved to fight! As individuals they displayed warmth and generosity, but when they crossed the threshold of the church or parish hall, they morphed into combatants spoiling for a fight. Clearly people who are busy fighting each other don't have time to do ministry. This was a church that needed to get to the bot-tom of the conflict and learn how to manage it.

Another common avoidance mechanism is the illusion of con-gregational poverty. Frequently congregations avoid doing min-istry by affecting the attitude, "We don't have enough money to do that." A church that is always pleading "poor mouth" as an excuse for not being involved in ministry needs to change its corporate culture of stewardship.

Ten Dumb Things Churches Do identified fear as the root cause of most problems in parish ministry. We would like to peel back that onion another layer. The fear that grips us is in large part *fear of the future*. But it is important to ask, what is the *present* to which we cling so tightly? What is so wonderful about where we are that makes it undesirable to go into the future?

For many church people, predictability is the most important element of their worship experience in church on Sunday morning. Our day-to-day lives are so full of change and uncertainty that perhaps it makes sense that people crave stability in their church lives. The problem with this is that the Gospel we read in churches every Sunday is about radical change and being prepared for the unpredictable. We cannot condone a sense of safety that is achieved at the price of ignoring the call to discipleship. The dissonance between the illusory comfort of the unchanging and the radical transformation promised by the Gospel is a point from which change can begin.

Church leaders know that it is not easy to lead a reluctant flock through change. Anthony Robinson offers five ways to engage a congregation in making adaptive changes:

- Ask questions that are sometimes annoying: "Why have you always done it that way?"
- Offer thoughtful critiques of emerging options: "What is the new non-denominational congregation down the street doing that brings in so many people, and what can we learn from it?"
- Disrupt the assumptions of the members; make a major change in the worship routine at least every now and then.
- Draw out conflict: "What can we learn from our disagreement over this seemingly intractable issue?"
- Challenge the norms: "Which norms are good and should be elevated to policy and which ones should be discarded because they are no longer appropriate?"[9]

While Jesus' message demands a corporate culture that values radical hospitality, deep spirituality, and a high level of commitment, many church members want only small doses of these challenges. In the worst cases, the church has become an instrument for affirming the status quo, not an agent for the difficult task of bringing about reconciliation in a divided and hurting world. Some of the other chapters in this book explore parts of the corporate culture that need to change for the Body of Christ to thrive in the twenty-first century.

Parish Nuts and Bolts
(and Other Hardware)

The next six chapters may seem familiar to readers of Ten Dumb Things That Churches Do *in that they are written in much the same format. While some of the chapter titles may resemble those in the previous book, you will see that the material is new. You could call these chapters* Six More Dumb Things Churches Do *if you like, but as before, there are a lot more than just six dumb things identified here.*

–4–

Money:
Where Is Your Heart, Really?

For where your treasure is, there your heart will be also.
—Matthew 6:21

If you really want to get a grip on your church's core values, just check out the budget. What percent of your budget goes to outreach? (The payment to the judicatory doesn't count toward outreach.) Does your church tithe by allocating at least 10 percent of its budget to ministries beyond its walls? What portion goes toward building maintenance? Is there any income generated from building use? What percent goes to personnel? And while we're on the subject, are the rates of pay for non-clergy staff competitive? For instance, is the parish secretary paid like a topnotch executive assistant or a fast food worker?

Some people get irritated when clergy bring up the subject of money. They claim it's not "spiritual" to talk about Mammon in church. Yet Jesus apparently talked about money a lot. He warned the rich young man that his wealth was an obstacle to his spiritual growth (Mark 10:17–22). He used the management of money as a teaching point in the Parable of the Talents (Matthew 25:14–30). The heart of his teachings about money is that we need to bring it into proper balance with other important values in life: "For where your treasure is, there your heart will be also." (Matthew 6:21)

If your congregation is genuinely on board with a set of core values and a core purpose, then presumably you know where your heart is. But is your treasure there also? The answer to where a church's heart really is can be found in the frequently hard realities of the church budget. In this chapter we will discuss the church's money under two headings: budget management and asset management.

Budget Management

The Money Path

The church's money is God's money. Or so we say. Yet when we pay our pledge, do we really *let go* of the money or do we leave some invisible strings attached? Do we have some expectations about how our pledge will be spent by the leaders of the church once it "becomes" God's money? Certainly we all carry some expectations about God's money, but hopefully those personal beliefs are consistent with the stated and operational beliefs of the church. We usually fail to remember that all money is God's money. God just lets us hold it and use it.

One parishioner was struggling with her attitudes about money, including her gifts to the church. When she received a windfall settlement of an insurance policy, she gave ten percent of the settlement to the church. Initially she had some concerns about how the money was to be used. Then, a day after she wrote the check, she told the pastor, "Use it as you see fit. I don't even want to know how you spend it. I am genuinely trying to give with no strings attached, the way Jesus did."

Giving "with no strings attached, the way Jesus did" challenges our usual approach to budget management. It might trivialize the process to inject the question "What would Jesus do?" every time the church treasurer wrote a check, but it would help the treasurer to see to it that all expenses are consistent with the core values and core purpose.

Let's take a look at how financial decisions are made in churches and who makes them. Whether we are talking about routine expenditures or the management of the endowment, it's important to ask: Who is empowered to make the decisions and who is supervising those who make decisions? How much discretion does the pastor (or the business manager) have to draw a check for any purpose? Do the individuals who are empowered to spend your church's money really understand finances? And regardless of who writes the checks, who is responsible for overseeing expenditures? Presumably the board and the treasurer have ultimate responsibility for managing financial decisions. The big question at the very bottom all these questions is this: *What is the connection between your core theology and your budget management?*

Assuming that you can identify how your theology relates to God's money, what safeguards do you have in place to ensure that the connection is maintained? Trust is a powerful invisible factor that affects a church's financial affairs. A strong pastor who has served a church capably for a number of years may have substantially more financial discretionary power than the hapless pastor whose predecessor was convicted of embezzlement. There's a different level of trust.

Another important factor that influences church finances is a financial decision-maker's personal perspective on money. For example, a layperson might approach church financial management like running a household frugally: you pay so much each month for the mortgage and other fixed expenses, and you look for coupons and bargains for everything else. Such economies are not necessarily sound stewardship, however. You might be able to buy a pair of shoes for $20 but you will have to replace them in six months. Applied to church finances, that sort of parsimony might result in hiring a janitor at minimum wage, then having to hire again within a few months.

The point is that it matters *who* makes the decisions because his or her trustworthiness and personal understanding of money comes into play. Ideally, your money managers will take on the core values and core purpose of the church, regardless of what they do at home.

Since the core is almost always linked to long-term goals, short-term bargains will rarely be cost effective.

Budget Formation

There are perhaps as many ways of assembling a church budget as there are churches. Whatever process a church uses, the values of the individuals involved usually bubble to the surface at budget meetings, sometimes to ill effect. In our view, one of the most horrifying things that can crop up in the budget-making process is a collective attitude that the world is a bad place where God is not present. The budget committee will never say this outright, but they will behave as if God is totally absent from the world of the church. The clergyperson trying to cope with these people may know that individually these people are the salt of the earth, generous givers, and genuinely devoted to the church. Yet when they meet as a budget committee, some dark aura forms around their heads. With apologies to bankers, we call this "banker mentality." Banker mentality requires that ministry represented by the money goes into neat piles or categories, that the final budget is a sacred document, and that little or no risk must be taken with God's money. What would Jesus make of that?

If you chair the finance committee for the next budget cycle, you may wish to begin by noting fixed costs such as debt service, utilities, and perhaps your judicatory assessment. Personnel costs also go into this category. While a church can exist without professional clergy, that is not really a viable long-term option in most circumstances.

The remainder of the budget will consist of program costs and other operating expenses such as printing and computer services. It may be tempting to save money by getting a deal on recycled paper or finding someone in the parish to handle your computer needs, but remember that you get what you pay for. The talented volunteer you get to do your word processing probably has a job that pays real money, which will mean handling the church's needs as time allows. And a serious meltdown can occur when the volunteer's personal computer crashes while she is preparing the Sunday bulletin.

It is a reality that the budget drawn up by the committee is not always fully supported by pledging and other income. Many churches face the necessity of adjusting the budget to fit pledged income. An under-funded budget often sets in motion a game of musical chairs for church programs, and any program chairperson who is not paying attention to the budget process may find that he or she no longer has a seat. When the budget has to be whittled down, the question is always hanging in the air: Is it better to under-fund all of the programs equally or to emphasize one at the expense of the others? The answer is to be found in the purpose statement of the parish. For example, if there is a clearly stated emphasis in the parish on Christian formation as opposed to outreach, it is good idea to fund Christian formation properly and look for some creative solutions for outreach like special fundraising or collaborative ministry with outside agencies.

Budget formation becomes easier as clarity about the big picture increases. If the church has a coherent strategic plan in place, the budget should reflect that future focus. The great ice hockey player Wayne Gretzky said that he was successful because he skated to where the puck *was going to be*. In the same way, a church needs to form a budget based not on where they are now but on *where they want to go*. This is not easy because many of the people in the system may not be around very long. The average tenure of pastors is seven to eight years. Board officers may serve two or three year terms. A budget committee may come together for only a few months of the year. So who is thinking about and taking responsibility for the budget five to ten years down the road?

Budget management is actually preceded by asset management, yet the fundamental question is the same: does this asset (or expense) contribute to the purpose and envisioned future of this church? If the answer is "yes," is it more or less important than other items? If the answer is "no," then how can the asset be converted to something that does contribute to the core purpose or envisioned future? For the many churches that are struggling just to hang on, it might make more sense to talk about "liability management" instead of "asset management." Nevertheless, stewardship is about being good stewards of God's bounty, not agonizing over the stuff we don't have.

The bottom line in church budget management is not so much about dollars and cents as it is about *risk*. As an example, there is a risk in having a paid youth minister when you do not already have a robust youth program. But is that risk greater or less than having no youth program at all? What *would* Jesus do?

Asset Management

The Real Estate

For most congregations, the church's real property is the largest and most important asset. The majority of parishioners believe that their congregation would be nothing without the church building, parish hall, and kitchen. Besides being a financial asset, a church's bricks and mortar give a congregation a sense of stability and permanence, the convenience of having facilities dedicated to their use, and a presence in the community.

One new congregation that met in the auditorium of the local elementary school discovered that they had a calling to outreach ministry. Their minimal expense for their worship space enabled them to have a generous outreach budget, and they developed a long-range plan to increase the outreach budget every year, with a goal of 35 percent of income going to outreach after ten years. Somewhere around the 20 percent level, however, they grew weary of meeting in a rented space and built a church to house their ministries. This caused their ministry priority to shift from outreach to church growth, a change that eventually split the parish and drove away the pioneering members with a passion for outreach. The new real estate the congregation has acquired contributes nothing to the old purpose of outreach, and given the building's size, configuration, and location, it is not likely ever to do so. The parish has lost its way and its members. We are not saying that congregations should not have real estate. Our point is that the real estate—every square foot of it—should contribute to the ministry.

Which has a greater influence over a church's budget: its real estate or its core purpose? Building maintenance and utilities, not to mention debt service, can be a substantial part of a church's expenses. But how does the real estate impact the church's income? How many square feet of space are idle five or six day a week? Is the space so specialized that it cannot be used for a purpose other than worship and Sunday school? If the church has stained glass windows, heavy pews bolted to the floor, and an immovable pulpit and altar, then it will be difficult to rent this space for anything besides worship or the occasional concert. Even so, a number of churches have successfully remodeled their interiors by removing the heavy sanctuary furnishings to make space for community theater, weddings, and homeless shelters. On Sundays the flexible space can be used for creative liturgy that may broaden the worship's appeal for newcomers.

Making structural changes to the sanctuary is not easy because many regard the worship space as sacred and immutable. Memorial gifts in the sanctuary such as stained glass windows, furnishings, and plaques create strong links to the congregation's past. Furthermore, property that is genuinely historic can draw visitors who, if given the right information, might come back on a Sunday to see what goes on. We should also note that property that is recognized as historic by local or national organizations may qualify for grants for building maintenance or restoration.

Nevertheless, radical changes are most likely to happen when there has been a catastrophe, such as a fire, or when the issue is forced: make changes or close. It all comes down to good stewardship: how can we make the best possible use of what God has given us? One church was inspired to take advantage of restoration to its main sanctuary following major fire damage. They decided to leave the pews out and use the worship space to expand their weekday lunch program. They still use the space for worship on the weekend, and their lunch program is now serving 1,200 meals a day. If we are fulfilling a declared purpose of making disciples by supporting a couple of hours of use per week of a worship space, then so be it. But let's be clear about the purpose and the cost attached. And let's also keep our eyes on the horizon so that we can plan ahead for changing purposes necessitated by changing conditions.

Congregations should review their real estate asset every so often, perhaps every five years, as a healthy for-profit business would do. Reviewing the property asset helps you determine whether you can improve or expand the ministry by using space more creatively or using it to produce income. Keep in mind that there are limits to the amount of rental income a church can have without risking loss of its tax-exempt status.

Endowments

Problems that arise in managing endowments are much the same, regardless of the size of the fund. The purpose of the endowment, like the purpose of everything else, is key. Is its purpose to help support the general operating budget, or a particular part of it, such as outreach? Is the purpose of the endowment consistent with the core values and core purpose of the parish? Some churches have a no-endowment policy because "Jesus wouldn't like it," so any large gifts the church receives go directly into ministry. Others have the policy that every special gift designated for a particular purpose or not goes into endowment. Experts on endowment management tend to avoid either of these two extreme positions.

So, what is the endowment for? (We'll exclude here all gifts that come with specific instructions attached, such as the endowment that underwrites trumpets at Easter or poinsettias at Christmas.) The Episcopal Church Foundation, whose mission includes helping churches with the management of endowments, suggests these purposes for special funds: outreach, new ministries, and capital improvements. All three of these purposes divert the benefits of an endowment away from the current congregation either to those in need beyond the parish or to the parish of the future.

1. **Outreach**. If the endowment is substantial, the management strategy could be similar to that of a foundation. There would be some guidelines for what kinds of projects the endowment will fund as well as a grant-making procedure.

2. **Capital Improvements**. Use of endowment funds for capital improvements is best restricted to future-oriented projects. Replacement of the gutters around the church may help to ensure the future of the building, but it should be regarded as maintenance. Any capital improvement from endowment funds should have to do with making the property more useable for a *new* ministry.

3. **New Ministries**. The church board could treat this category in the same manner as outreach, i.e., on a grant basis. The endowment could fund a new ministry in full for one year, then provide decreasing amounts of support for several more years, so long as evaluations remain positive. The new ministry would gradually either move into the operating budget or spin off as a separate non-profit organization. And if the ministry is not meant to be, it will die a natural death.

Of course, it's easy enough to think of ways to make end runs around the rules. Just as most any repair could imaginatively be labeled a "capital improvement," so the payment to the judicatory could be called "outreach," and hiring an administrative assistant could be called a "new ministry." It's up to the church to be honest about its motives.

One church with an aging membership decided to work hard to build up the endowment. The membership had been declining for years, and the board saw the future endowment as a hedge against the shrinking number of pledges. The unspoken implication of this strategy was that the parish of the future would consist of a handful of elderly parishioners with a budget covered entirely by an endowment, a sort of pension fund for the congregation.

What is the theology for such a ministry? Arts organizations crave endowments that will free them from the burden of annual fundraising. But do you want your congregation to be free of the *opportunity* to participate in the stewardship of God's abundance? There is a cost for discipleship, including a financial one.

Stoking the Endowment

What motivates people to give money to endowments, either while they are living or through their wills? Some reasons are:

- The gift is an extension of pledging
- Gratitude for ministry received
- Interest in a particular aspect of ministry such as music, spiritual retreats, etc.
- The desire to create a legacy—leaving a part of themselves behind in order to benefit others

If you want to build up your endowment, you may approach people based on any of these reasons for giving. They will probably want to know:

- how the money will be managed, and
- how specific they should be about what the money is for.

Preparing to build an endowment requires a congregation to think through its values, purpose, and envisioned future. Before spending a lot of time and effort on planned giving, be sure to check the values and purposes of the congregation and of the endowment.

Here are a few tips for building the endowment:

- Get over your fear of talking about money.
- Talk about money positively—it is a sign of God's abundance.
- Remember, hoarding money is just as sinful as spending it recklessly.
- Offer church members well-thought-out avenues for planned giving.
- Thank all donors with a handwritten note.
- Publicly celebrate God's abundance.

One final note: All of these ideas about money depend upon really, we mean *really*, believing that it is God's money and that we are simply servants who have a hand in the care and distribution of it. The bottom line is not profit or loss; the bottom line is ministry.

–5–

Structure:
Why Size Matters

Moses heard the people weeping throughout their families, all at the entrances of their tents. Then the Lord became very angry, and Moses was displeased. So Moses said to the Lord, 'Why have you treated your servant so badly? Why have I not found favor in your sight, that you lay the burden of all this people on me? . . . I am not able to carry all this people alone, for they are too heavy for me . . . So the Lord said to Moses, 'Gather for me seventy of the elders of Israel . . . and I will take some of the spirit that is on you and put it on them; and they shall bear the burden of the people along with you so that you will not bear it all by yourself. (Numbers 11: 10–17)

Theologian Howard Thurman told the story of a train journey that took him across the vast expanse of Texas. The train stopped across a highway at a place called Big Sandy. Looking out the window Thurman noticed a huge billboard advertising a local business. It read: "Five highways meet here. Four chances to go wrong. Ask us."

There are lots of ways to go wrong in parish ministry, but possibly the most common errors made by clergy or lay leaders are in the area of structure and management. Effective ministry requires the implementation of an organizational structure and management style that fits the congregation.

The appropriate administrative structure depends largely on the size of the church. We have adopted Arlin Rothauge's widely used and useful classification of churches published in *Sizing Up a Congregation for New Member Ministry* (Episcopal Church Center, 1983). The basic idea is that the size of a church as measured by average Sunday attendance ("ASA") determines the fundamental organizational scheme for the church. Obviously a small-membership church with a single pastor and a part-time secretary operates differently than a large-membership church with a large staff and several weekly services.

The key variable in the organizational schemes of different sized churches is *how the members of the congregation and the pastor relate to each other* (the last column in the chart below).

Avg. Sunday Attendance	Key Leaders	Self Identity	Organizational Scheme	What the Pastor does . . .	How members/ pastor relate
Family < 50	Long-time members	"Family chapel"	None needed	What the (key) members want	Directly
Pastoral 50–150	The pastor	"One big family"	Pastor makes all decisions	Everything	Directly
Program 150–350	The pastor, staff, and key lay leaders	What we *do*	Pastor makes most decisions; consults with staff and lay leaders as needed	Almost everything	May relate directly to pastor; some will relate to associate pastor or particular lay ministers
Corporate or Resource >350	The senior pastor (and staff)	"Big important church," "cultural/arts center," "activists," etc.	Collection of departments with staff and/or lay leadership for each department	With vestry, "keeper of the vision"; supervises staff; much preaching; some pastoral work	Members look to senior pastor for leadership and spiritual guidance. Pastoral care comes mostly from staff and trained laity
Cathedral	Same as Corporate	Multiple centers of worship or foci	Same as corporate but more division by sub-congregation or demographic	Same as Corporate	Usually each congregation identifies with particular staff member

With apologies to Rothauge, we have added to his matrix a fifth category, which we have designated "Cathedral." This is the result of a pattern Philip noticed in one church where he served as interim rector. Here's what happened.

St. Swithin's In-the-Swamp grew steadily through the 1970s and 1980s as the town's population swelled, increasing from a pastoral size to a program size church. Because the rector during this time was an exceptional pastor, everyone continued to think and operate like the members of a pastoral church, even though the church had outgrown that model. When he retired, a new rector instituted some structural elements appropriate to the program size church, such as assigning each member of the vestry to function as a liaison to one of the program committees. Congregants nonetheless continued to think of themselves as members of a pastoral church who each had a direct relationship with the rector.

A principal reason this pastoral mindset remained firmly in place was to be found in the unique Sunday worship schedule the church had evolved. Like many Episcopal churches, the parish had a traditional 8 AM Rite I Holy Eucharist and a Rite II Holy Eucharist at 10:30 AM. The remarkable thing about their worship schedule was that they *also* had at 10:30 AM a service with contemporary music and liturgy, which drew an equal number of worshipers. A fourth service had been added on Saturday evenings. Each service was distinctive enough that few worshipers crossed over from one sub-congregation to the other. The average attendance by service was:

Saturday 5 PM	35
Sunday 8 AM	65
Sunday 10:30 AM	150
Sunday 10:30 AM Contemporary	150

In effect, then, St. Swithin's had *four* congregations, each of which was either pastoral or family size. While congregants occasionally came together for parish-wide educational and social events, social ties were based on these distinct congregations and most people knew and associated primarily with the people in their own group. At the first gathering of the new Strategic Planning Team and

Search Committee, some members actually met each other for the first time!

A second factor that prevented St. Swithin's from recognizing its true larger church identity was that their pastoral size self-image had simply never been challenged. This was despite their having grown out of this category at least twenty years previously.

The disparity between the church's pastoral size self-image and its much larger actual size made the staff's task like trying to squeeze a size six shoe onto a size twelve foot. It created several problems, the primary one being the high burnout rate of the clergy. The congregation's pastoral church expectation that everyone would have direct access to the pastor was obviously impossible to meet, not only for the rector, but even for the rector and assisting clergy combined. Fortunately, one element of the program church that did operate here was that some members regarded one of the assisting clergy as their primary pastor. Given the size of the parish, however, even the program model was inadequate to cover the pastoral needs of the congregation.

Another major problem was that the existing organizational structure was weak and poorly defined. This large and rather complex church was operating with a pastoral church scheme, in which the pastor does just about everything, with some staff and lay assistance. This resulted in vague job descriptions for a staff of twelve and hazy lines of accountability for staff and lay leaders alike.

It is critical to get the appropriate organizational scheme in place to handle the present needs of the church. It is also important to manage the expectations of the members. This requires patience. If the church has been operating with an inadequate administrative model, it takes repeated explanation—and possibly several years—to realign the expectations of members with the reality of the organization. The staff must also work diligently to generate enough small groups and committees to fit the organizational scheme of the resource size church.

In their parish survey, St. Swithin's members made it clear that they sought a "spiritual leader" in their next rector. But did that mean that respondents wanted a spiritual leader for their particular sub-congregation? Or, if they wanted a spiritual leader for the whole parish, was that desire accompanied by an awareness that they might have to give up something, namely their separation from one another?

With the assistance of an astute consultant, Philip determined that St. Swithin's was, in fact, operating something like a cathedral. In this model (the last row on the chart), there may be any number of worship services, with no need or desire to make them into a single congregation. These separate worshiping groups are probably sufficiently diverse that this would be an uphill battle in any case. In a cathedral, the dean, as symbolic head of the church, relates to all of the congregations to some degree, while the staff may be organized in such a way that each sub-congregation identifies primarily with one of the clergy. Another possibility is for individual parts of the ministry—such as pastoral care, Christian formation, or outreach—to be directed by professionals who are visible to the whole church. This model is viable so long as the "cathedral" church has sufficient staff to make it work. Dr. Robert Schuller's Crystal Cathedral boasts a staff that handles pastoral care for more than ten thousand members. Hardly anyone in that congregation has a personal relationship with Dr. Schuller, but everyone knows that there is a staff person who knows their name and the names of their children.

Some people are energized by the array of choices offered by a cathedral church, such as worship services in different styles or different languages and a smorgasbord of educational programs and volunteer opportunities. Yet for many others there remains the longing to have a personal relationship with *the* pastor, as their family had in the church where they grew up. After all, a substantial majority of mainline churches in the United States are family and pastoral size. Smaller churches exist for a reason, and it is not just that these churches have failed to grow. The family or pastoral church is a comfortable size for people who want that direct relationship to the pastor.

Unity, Not Uniformity

There is no question that our national population is becoming increasingly diverse. Throughout the United States, communities large and small have become magnets for groups of immigrants from all over the world. Young people have little interest in cultural uniformity and their friendships cut across ethnic and cultural boundaries. It follows that unless churches can genuinely support a corporate culture of unity in diversity rather than insisting on one of uniformity, we can expect continued diminishing membership—and eventual closure—of our churches.

A key feature of the pastoral size church, apart from the members' direct relationship to the pastor, is the members' relationship to one another. Let's take a fictional pastoral size church with an ASA (average Sunday attendance) of about 100. We'll call it Bypass Community Church. It's pretty well established that about one-third of a church's members attend services on a given Sunday, so we can project that Bypass Community Church actually has about 300 members. This number comprises about 130 families, including those who come only occasionally.

Using "the 20/80 rule," meaning that in any organization, 20 percent of the people do 80 percent of the work, we can estimate that at Bypass, about 25 families haul most of the freight. It's also a good bet that the people who make up the active core of the church know each other quite well.

It is also likely that this core group at Bypass Community Church is not very culturally diverse. There may be some generational spread, perhaps some ethnic diversity, and possibly some range of opinion on key church issues. But for the most part, uniformity among the core 20 percent reflects similar uniformity for the rest of the congregation.

Of course it would be a distortion to say that all family and pastoral size parishes are homogeneous. Plenty of them are not. We should not assume, either, that diversity necessarily increases as a church's membership grows into the program and resource size range. Even so, it is possible for a congregation to grow into diversity. The way to create a potential for increased diversity in a church of *any* size is to put before the parish the idea of *unity* in place of *uniformity*.

In the chapter on corporate culture we suggested that a newcomer attempting to enter the congregation is scoping out the corporate culture by asking—at least subconsciously—such questions as:

- Are these my people?
- Do I fit in here?

The newcomer must discern whether he or she matches up with the corporate culture, could adapt to it, or needs to exit and find another community.

What does it mean for a church's corporate culture to support diversity? We have seen that one way to sustain diversity is through the cathedral model, an organization large enough to separate people into different congregations according to age, liturgical preference, marital status, or other demographic factors. But what of the church that does not have the resources to staff a variety of liturgical offerings every week? Is it still possible to build diversity in a single worshiping congregation? Yes, *if the corporate culture genuinely values diversity*, that is, if both stated beliefs and operational beliefs support diversity.

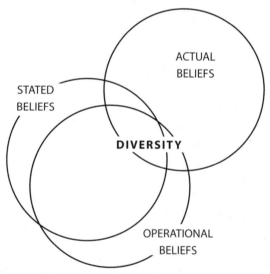

In this parish, **stated beliefs** and **operational beliefs** are well aligned, however **actual beliefs** may vary. Diversity (as represented by the non-aligned actual beliefs) is possible because the members believe that corporate culture (as represented by stated and operational beliefs) is more important to them than their personal beliefs. In time, it is likely that actual beliefs will overlap more with stated and operational beliefs.

"Who's in Charge?"

A structural issue that is causing trouble in many mainline churches is ambiguity about who is in charge. In hierarchically organized denominations, such as Episcopal or Lutheran, lines of authority extend outward and upward from the congregation to an executive or bishop or council, either regional or national. But American culture contains a powerful counterforce that challenges the hierarchical lines of authority of these denominations, namely, the belief in democracy. The town-meeting democracy instituted in colonial times by the Puritans who settled in New England has become widely understood as "the way we do things in this country," and government by the will of the majority has been slowly gaining strength in our hierarchical churches. Even our Roman Catholic brothers and sisters have learned to sort through Papal statements for what is and is not acceptable to them individually. Episcopalians kind of like it when the bishop comes to visit wearing fancy vestments and walking in procession with a big shepherd's crook, but at the same time they increasingly rely on local options to bail them out of having to go along with whatever happened at the last General Convention. Stated beliefs, operational beliefs, and actual beliefs may be quite separate in the area of "who is in charge."

Nevertheless, the trend is clearly towards local autonomy. More and more people are members of non-denominational churches that owe no allegiance to any external authority, while those in denominational churches pay less and less attention to what is going on in the denomination. Young people, who have little or no interest in the machinations of creaky old institutions, wonder why debates about such topics as sexuality generate so much excitement among their elders.

Even in a genuinely democratic polity, such as that of the United Church of Christ and other historically congregational denominations, it is not possible to vote on *every* decision that comes before the church. Representative democracy operates when church members elect leaders whom they expect to lead them along paths that may have been discussed in the election process. Elected leaders must balance listening to the *vox populi* with leading the people in the direction the leader feels called to go. More about this in Chapter 6.

The authority dynamic operating between parish and denomination depends to some extent upon denominational polity, that is, whether the denomination has a hierarchical authority structure like Episcopal churches or a "bottom upwards" system like the United Church of Christ. The size of a parish may also be a factor. Large churches may tend to ignore the denomination even though they pay their denominational pledge. Even the geographical location of the church may affect how closely it follows denominational or local authority. We have noticed that churches that are located at a great geographical distance from regional offices sometimes feel that the denomination doesn't know or care about them, and go their own way.

Ultimately, denominations need to do the same thing parishes do, that is, examine their core beliefs, core purpose, and envisioned future. While a denomination's core beliefs are probably stable, their core purpose may need to be overhauled, which in turn will lead to changes in the envisioned future. Doing this hard work could revitalize our mainline denominations and give them a new reason for being.

Management Style

Of course, it's entirely possible to have the right organizational scheme for the size of a congregation and still have a disaster. Alban Institute studies show that most pastorates that fail in the first couple of years do so because clergy and laity have not correctly matched their management styles.

The management style of clergy and lay leaders can be located somewhere on the chart in Chapter 6 (see page 94), which offers a simplified way of looking at the problem. We emphasize that there is no real right or wrong to any of these management styles. To paraphrase Ecclesiastes, there is a time to be passive and a time to be active, a time to work alone and a time to work with others. The trick is in knowing *when* to do which one.

Flexibility is particularly necessary in the administration of a church. In a business setting, it is important for managers to be consistent, or at least predictable, in their management style. A manager who favors a team approach one day will confuse the workers by being highly directive the next day. However, in a church setting, the wise leader working with different constituencies learns how to shift gears, even several times a day. For example, a senior pastor may have one management style with the staff, another with the board, another with the youth group, another with the women's group, and so on. The wisdom to know which approach works best with each constituency must be developed through a certain amount of trial and error.

A new pastorate can fail quickly when the management style the laity expects is different from the management style the new pastor actually employs. At Little Brown Church, the pastor managed the church from a position well over on the left side of the chart. That is, she took a back seat to the lay leaders, helping them when they wanted help, preaching good sermons, making pastoral calls, but otherwise not doing much management at all. The people liked her enough and were energetic enough that they simply filled the management vacuum with their own energy and talent. During her tenure, the church had a successful capital campaign and building project, maintained solid programs, and experienced growth. (When she retired, the parish engaged an untrained interim pastor who did even better at relationships, but did little additional direct leadership.) The next pastor was called on the strength of his perceived ability to grow the church. What the search committee missed, however, was the fact that this person was highly directive—that is, his style was well to the right and low on the chart. In short, the two pastors could not have been more different. The people bristled at the commands of the new pastor, and trouble ensued.

There is some connection between church size and the pastoral management style that will work. A family size church is usually run by a matriarch or patriarch, a long-time member who has been instrumental in the leadership of the church for a generation or more. A pastor who comes into this situation and tries to be a team builder may be indulged, but he or she will eventually be "trained" to do things the matriarch's way. The pastoral size church usually invests substantial authority in the pastor since he or she has to do so much to keep the place going. A passive style of leadership in this kind of church may simply cause the church to fall asleep and spiral downwards toward death. Program and resource size churches require flexible leaders who know how to read a situation and respond with the right mixture of direction, instruction, helping, and serving. Anyone who has been a parent is familiar with the necessity of changing gears as one's child grows. Similarly, people in a church grow (and sometimes regress), and everyone is at a different stage of development. What is required of the leader is what family systems theory calls being "a non-anxious presence with a high level of self-differentiation." That means simply that the pastor is not easily ruffled, and trusts in her skills and God's grace enough that she can be patient while people struggle with a problem.

Leadership:
Servant Leader . . . or Just Another Boss?

Keep watch over yourselves and over all the flock, of which the Holy Spirit has made you overseers, to shepherd the church of God that he obtained with the blood of his own Son. I know that after I have gone, savage wolves will come in among you, not sparing the flock. Some even from your own group will come distorting the truth in order to entice the disciples to follow them. Therefore be alert.

—Acts 20:28–31a

As members of the church, we know that the Holy Spirit endows each of us with diverse talents and that the Spirit works through us in various ways, including some that may take us by surprise. However, the health of the church as a body requires more than reliance on the divine grace of the Spirit or the sincere belief and firm commitment of its members. It also requires some understanding of leadership.

The Woes of the Nominating Committee

It was standard practice at Stuckwood Community Church for board members nearing the end of their term of office to serve as the nominating committee for candidates for board vacancies at the next election. The departing board members tried to think of people who had not previously served but who showed commitment to the church and had some skill that would be helpful to the board. They drew up a list of fifteen names, hoping to find among them eight good candidates who would be willing to run for the four vacant board positions.

But when the nominating committee contacted the proposed candidates, not a single one could be persuaded to run for the board! They gave such reasons as:

- I'm already doing several volunteer jobs for the church.
- I don't feel I'm qualified.
- I just volunteered to be den mother for my son's Scout troop.

Two other reasons offered were especially distressing to the nominating committee:

- I don't like the people who are on the board.
- I don't want the responsibility.

Churches are not alone in the difficulty of finding good leadership. Recruiting good people to serve on the board is a challenge for any non-profit organization. Serving on a board is a major assignment when undertaken seriously. Nominees know going in that in addition to serving on the board they will be expected to be lead financial donors and will likely be asked to chair a committee.

So what did the Stuckwood nominating committee do? They put a note in the church newsletter asking for volunteers to run for the vacant board positions. That produced two candidates: a major donor who did not like the pastor very much and a member who attended worship regularly but never participated in any other church activity. The committee agreed that the two self-selected candidates would not be good board members.

Now the nominating committee was really in trouble! Their solution was to go back to the first fifteen people on their list and tell them that unless they ran for election, the undesirable candidates would most likely be on the board. You can see what kind of mess this could lead to, with the wrong people serving on the board for the wrong reasons.

Why are people so reluctant to lead? There may be many possible answers arising from such things as differences in individual personalities. What we want to focus on in this chapter are common institutional roadblocks for potential leaders in the church. The question we would pose is this: What aspects within the organization keep good leaders (or potentially good leaders) from taking on positions of responsibility? Put another way, what is there in the corporate culture of a church that gets in the way of leadership?

Lack of Trust

Lack of trust between members and lay leaders is a primary obstacle for potential leaders. A congregation may have developed a pattern of not trusting its leaders based upon some real or perceived negative history. Do you frequently hear statements like these?

- The board doesn't communicate with us (the members).
- The board is too tight with the money.
- The board is too loose with the money.
- All the board ever thinks about is money.
- The board does whatever the pastor wants.
- The board doesn't respect the pastor.
- The same people are always on the board.
- There's no one on the board under sixty years of age (or fifty or forty, etc.).

Comments like these indicate that some members of the congregation don't view the board as trustworthy. Disgruntled members who believe that the board does not consider their point of view may undermine board decisions, effectively cutting the board off at the knees, meanwhile giving themselves permission to go their own merry way. In an environment that consistently undermines its leaders, only very brave or very foolish people are willing to be leaders. A pervasive, long-lasting lack of trust in a church is difficult to change.

In some churches, the lack of trust that hinders leadership is directed not at the board but toward the pastor. This crippling problem frequently exists in congregations with a history of pastors who have abused their office. In one church, two pastors in a row engaged in messy and public sexual misconduct. In another, four pastors over two generations engaged in behavior that necessitated their early retirement or departure under duress. These congregations whose clergy betrayed their trust came to believe that all clergy are untrustworthy. Their members made statements such as:

- The pastor doesn't communicate with us (the members).
- The pastor is too tight with the money.
- The pastor is too loose with the money.
- All the pastor ever talks about is money.
- The pastor does whatever the board wants.
- The pastor doesn't respect the board or anyone else.
- The pastor doesn't understand us.

Betrayed trust is exceedingly difficult to repair. Repairing broken trust in a congregation, whether the problem is located in the clergy or the laity or both, requires great patience and diligence. This careful rebuilding process must start with the paid leaders. The pastor and other professional staff should be effective leaders themselves. Most importantly, they need to be skilled in training others to lead. (In the language of family systems theory, the church must have clergy with a high level of self-differentiation who can be a positive presence and pull the congregation into a higher level of self-differentiation.) A genuinely trustworthy pastor who has some ability in leadership training can begin training board members and other laypersons already in leadership positions. That training should help the leaders to develop important skills such as how to run a meeting, gain consensus, listen and guide, communicate decisions, and evaluate openly. With this kind of instruction, trust that begins to grow within the leadership team will in time extend to others in the congregation.

One key element of leadership that is not easily taught is the ability to withstand negative criticism. Of course, it is always possible that someone in the parish will not like some aspect of any particular decision leaders make. Many of us tend to take all criticism personally. A person who perceives any criticism as a personal attack is likely to move into a defensive posture, with such verbal responses as, "My way or the highway," or "Like it or leave it." An effective leader, however, is able to listen to criticism without taking it personally. It's crucial to remember that the criticism is not about the person, it's about the decision. It's also important to keep in mind that humility is an admirable quality in a leader. Sometimes it may be appropriate to compromise or change course. Humility, openness, and honesty build trust. Arrogance, belligerence, and defensiveness weaken trust.

Many of our churches are blessed with the presence of skilled professionals who are willing to bring their talents to leadership roles in the church. It is important to recognize that while leadership in the church in some respects resembles leadership in the secular world, it also is different in some important ways. Parker Palmer reminds us that, at best, leadership arises from our spiritual depths.

> The problem is that people rise to leadership in our society by a tendency towards extroversion, which means a tendency to ignore what is going on inside themselves. Leaders rise to power in our society by operating very competently and effectively in the external world, sometimes at the cost of internal awareness. I'm suggesting that leaders . . . may tend to be people who screen out the inner consciousness. . . . I have met many leaders whose confidence in the external world is so high that they regard the inner life as illusory, as a waste of time, as a magical fantasy trip into a region that doesn't even exist. But the link between leadership and spirituality calls us to re-examine that denial of inner life.[10]

When we learn to lead from that deep interior place, the fears, sorrows, and disappointments that we all experience are transformed by the grace of God into wisdom. Leadership can be part of our spiritual development.

The Art of Church Leadership

Management Style

Here is a chart from *Ten Dumb Things Churches Do*:

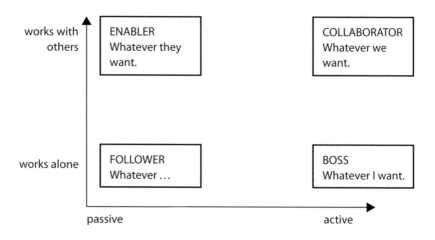

Whenever we work with a church board or congregation, we ask them to locate a spot on this chart that they think represents the leadership style of their current pastor (or would like their next pastor to have). If it is a church board, we ask them where they think they are on the chart and where they believe the congregation perceives them to be. This exercise is useful because it helps to identify the discrepancies between expectation and reality that result in disappointment and often head towards conflict.

The St. Martha's Guild at Stuckwood Community Church was a powerful women's organization that for many years had raised a lot of money and generously disbursed it around the parish for various expenses, especially for capital improvements. That was all fine, except for the fact that the guild operated independently and did not necessarily disburse funds in accordance with the priorities of the church board. Various pastors had handled this situation in different ways. Some went to the guild regularly with requests for unusual or unexpected expenses. Other pastors left them alone to do as they pleased, trusting that whatever they did would be beneficial to the parish, even if it was not an official priority.

St. Martha's Guild's purchase of a new carpet for the parish hall was illustrative of the way things worked at Stuckwood. The guild, which often provided food for church events in the parish hall, was aware that the carpet had become stained and shabby. So they decided to replace the carpet and sent a letter informing the church board of their intentions. The letter, which described the carpet project as a done deal, was accompanied by a set of instructions and policies regarding the new carpet, including the banning from the room of all red juice products except for wine. The guild had thoughtfully selected a *café au lait* colored carpet to minimize the impact of coffee spills. Everyone on the board thought this was business as usual, except for the newly arrived pastor, who wondered aloud what the mechanism for this five-figure expenditure might be and exactly who was supposed to enforce the rules about the serving of beverages. The answers were not easy to find, as Stuckwood had a rather loose system of authority and accountability, a void in which the guild operated as a law unto itself.

The men's ministry was similarly independent, possibly borrowing its management style from the guild. Once this kind of autonomy gets going, it is hard to rein groups in to a common purpose. Some of Stuckwood's pastors who had tried to coordinate these groups had run afoul of the congregation's expectation of a laissez faire management style, while others simply took the path of least resistance and went along with the independent operations of the various groups. The absence of coordinated leadership made for an energetic but somewhat chaotic parish.

While there is virtue in having strong, clear lay leadership of organizations within a parish, note that they would all be well over on the right hand-side of the chart. This clearly creates problems for a pastor who would like to occupy some of the same space on the chart. The pastor who wants to realign the lay leadership so that they all head in a unified direction will need to work with care to accomplish that goal. Here's what Stuckwood's organizational chart would look like:

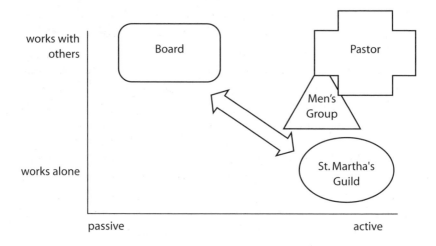

The pastor may be able to relate to all of these constituencies, but the distance between St. Martha's Guild and the board is a difficult gap to close. While the board may be somewhere over to the right of the chart when making budget decisions, they will always be to the left of St. Martha's Guild. In this case, St. Martha's Guild will be fully engaged with strategic planning priorities adopted by the board only by the grace of God.

Marked differences in leadership style from one pastor to another can also create problems for a church. Here is fairly extreme example of a disparity of management style. Unfortunately, it is not uncommon (see next page).

In Chapter 5 we told the story of Little Brown Church that had an enabling type of pastor on the left side of the chart, followed by a highly directive pastor positioned on the opposite side of the chart. The interim pastor was more like pastor #1 than pastor #2. The congregation experienced whiplash in the transition from the laid-back style they had previously experienced to the directive style of pastor #2. Apart from the differing management styles of the three pastors, several factors contributed to this mess:

- Church members did not accurately perceive their situation while they were in the search process.

- The interim did not move out of his area of comfort as a manager to expose the congregation to some other possibilities for management style.
- The pastors themselves were likely unaware of their management styles and the effects of their actions.

The resulting sudden extreme change in management style rocked the congregation from top to bottom.

The kind of calamity that befell Little Brown Church can be avoided by understanding how things work in your church and how you want them to work in the future. In the case of the wayward internal organizations of the previous example, the solution is to get everyone pulling in the same direction. If the church has undergone a thorough self-examination, has considered their corporate culture, and can articulate their core values, they should be well on the way to narrowing gaps that may appear in their management style chart.

The chart enables us to visually identify different kinds of leaders with differing skills. Some leaders are good at setting boundaries, saying "no" when appropriate, and moving the troops in the right direction. Another kind of leader may have good skills for listening and being able to build consensus. B. Joseph White writes about these two

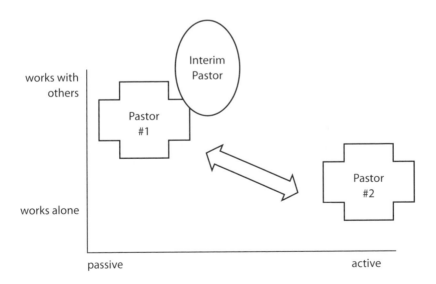

kinds of leader in his book *The Nature of Leadership*. He calls them "reptiles" and "mammals." White makes the important point that the best leaders can invoke both reptilian and mammalian qualities—firm and soft—as needed. Outstanding leaders can do first one technique and then another, as the situation requires. The reality of parish life is that different leadership styles are appropriate in different times and places. The art of parish management lies in knowing when to be passive or active and when to be directive or collaborative.

Identifying Lay Leaders

St. Gwendolyn's was in the process of calling a new pastor. The staff recognized that a lack of unity in this resource size parish was causing problems in several areas, including pledging and budgeting. The parish needed consensus about its future direction. The staff decided to engage the lay leaders in solving the problem. The clergy identified three categories of leaders. "Founders" were those who had been members for thirty or more years or whose family roots in the 250-year-old parish extended back for generations. "Donors" were major pledgers who provided significant financial support. The third group, "Worker Bees," were the core members who serve on the committees and did the many volunteer jobs around the parish. Of course, many people fit two or all three categories.

Leaders were invited to a series of gatherings where they were seated at assigned tables, with groupings deliberately assorted to assure a cross-section of members. The most important part of the first meeting was conversation around the tables about the essential issues facing the parish as a whole. Many people reported afterward that they had met members of the church they had not previously known, even though all were leaders of one kind or another. The program for the next two meetings was to empower the leaders through leadership training and coaching in how to talk about the church they loved.

In your own church you can identify leaders according to these categories or others you find appropriate, such as generational leaders. Every church has Donors and Worker Bees. While some people may be in both categories, leaders who are in one group may harbor some resentment towards members of the other. A Donor, for example, may not like the way the food pantry is operated. Worker Bees may wish that those who are contributing heavily to the organ repair fund would give more to the food pantry. But of course *all* of these people are needed to make a complete ministry. All profess to be Christians, all are leaders, and all have some degree of loyalty to the organization. Imagine what might happen if they talked to each other and strategized together. You might have a parish full of leaders all leading in the same direction!

Leadership as Ministry

The church is unique when it comes to leadership issues. Leadership that works in the corporate world, government, or non-profits certainly has some relationship to the church. What is different is that church leadership is part of the ministry itself, not solely a function that makes a business go. Apart from other functions of organizational leadership, the church leader, as we see it, must always consider how a decision or an action helps to build the Body of Christ. Church leadership is not about *doing things for others*, it's about *helping others do things for each other.*

The Interim:
It's Not a Vacation

Then Moses ordered Israel to set out from the Red Sea, and they went into the wilderness of Shur. They went for three days in the wilderness and found no water. When they came to Marah, they could not drink the water of Marah because it was bitter. . . . And the people complained against Moses, saying, 'What shall we drink?' He cried out to the Lord; and the Lord showed him a piece of wood; he threw it into the water, and the water became sweet.

—Exodus 15:22–25

The interim time between pastors can seem like a thirsty trek in the wilderness. If you are a lay leader of a church that is on such a journey, or is about to start, you may find yourself longing for the Promised Land, or at least reminiscing fondly about the security of the old pastorate. Know that you will get there in God's good time and that you will face significant kvetching no matter how healthy your church is.

The interim is a valuable time in the life of a church, but not necessarily an easy time. While denominational judicatories continue to try new ways to enhance the quality of the interim period or to shorten it, there are still plenty of dumb things churches do in the time between pastors.

A trapeze artist was asked what it was like to go somersaulting through the air from the trapeze bar to the man on the other trapeze who caught her. She answered that tumbling through space and finding the catcher was fairly easy—there wasn't time to think. The hard part was letting go of the trapeze in the first place!

In transitions between pastors, churches have a lot of time to think—maybe too much time. It used to be that all that was expected of an interim pastor was to keep the basic elements of parish life going—worship, pastoral calling, counseling, and programs that were already up and running. The norm was that this period lasted only a few months while a search committee interviewed candidates for the vacant position. However, the interim period has become much longer, now averaging from twelve to twenty-four months.

Three factors have contributed to this lengthening. First, judicatory officials have learned that a key part of a successful transition is helping the congregation to cope with the past, whether positive or negative, and that takes time. Second, church officials have learned that a search process is likely to be more successful if the church takes the time not only to turn the page on their past but also to look closely at who they are, what values they use to make decisions, what mechanisms they have for making decisions, and where they think God may call them to go. Third, it takes a certain amount of time for a search committee to achieve consensus on the qualities they seek in a new pastor and to discern them in candidates, first from pieces of paper and then from live interviews. A history of conflict in the church can lengthen the process even further.

If your church is between pastors, what will you do with all this interim time? We will explore the potential value of the interim time by looking at the three key tasks of interim ministry: celebrating and healing the past, keeping the ministry going, and preparing the way for the new pastor. At the end of the chapter we will take a look at a few specific issues in the search process.

Celebrating the Past

Pastor Goodbody is leaving your church and you are feeling abandoned. Pastor Goodbody may have baptized your children, visited you in the hospital, or even saved your marriage, but he is not God. Pastor Goodbody is a human being who feels that it is time to minister in a new setting or retire. Pastor Goodbody is not the last good pastor out there, but that is not what is on your mind when he announces his departure. You and many others in the parish feel a special connection to this individual, even if you were never in his home except for the Christmas Open House. After all, it seemed like he was speaking only to you Sunday after Sunday. While he may seem to be irreplaceable, he will be replaced. So celebrate the end of Pastor Goodbody's wonderful ministry in your church and let him, and yourself, move on to a new relationship.

One more thing. Do him and your next pastor a favor: do not call up Pastor Goodbody when you need any of the following:

- Another child baptized
- A wedding
- Counseling for a spiritual crisis
- Someone to complain to about the new pastor
- A fourth for bridge (unless he has retired from the ministry and made it clear that he will be there to play bridge, not to talk about the church)

Here are some tips on how your church can appropriately celebrate the past:

1. **The Program.** If Pastor Goodbody's ministry included some wildly successful program, like a weekly Bible study or a food closet, by all means honor him by keeping the program going, but allow it to take a new shape. Your new pastor will have a different way of doing Bible study or may be interested in Habitat for Humanity rather than the food closet.

2. **The History.** If your church has had a series of Pastor Goodbody's and is something of a fixture in the community, then you have HISTORY. History, like the departing pastor, is something to celebrate and not to worship. Celebrate a special anniversary date or your patronal feast. Have a blowout party for the sesquicentennial anniversary of the church's founding. Just keep one thing in mind: history is not ministry.

3. **The Staff.** No matter how large or small your church may be, remember to honor the staff members who are still there. You

need them now more than ever. While you're celebrating, celebrate their ministries, too, so that they know you want them in your future.

Letting Go of the Past

The pioneers who settled the western United States often began their journeys with wagons full of furniture and personal treasures they hoped to use in their new life beyond the western mountains. But the long, arduous journey forced them to discard any item that wasn't absolutely necessary for survival. By the time they reached Oregon, they had jettisoned pianos and ancestral portraits beside the rocky trail and burnt the rest for firewood when they were desperate. They simply couldn't make the journey weighed down by unnecessary baggage.

What baggage is your church carrying that weighs you down? The interim period is a time for dealing with it. In some ways it's like cleaning out a long-neglected closet. You are likely to generate several bags of stuff to throw out or give away. As you work your way to the back of the closet, you may find things you thought you had lost. You might want to try a new organizational scheme for the closet. The end result will be that every time you open the closet, you will be delighted that you can find what you need, and you will have a pile of garbage to take out.

During the interim at St. Fungo's, a resource size church, the business manager was cleaning out some files when she came across a contract for what appeared to be a satellite congregation. We'll call it St. Goofy's. It seems that in the dim recesses of history, St. Fungo's had spawned a congregation literally on the "other side of the tracks." Over time, however, attendance dwindled until the congregation consisted of a single family, who paid one dollar in rent to St. Fungo's but did not pledge.

The Board of St. Fungo's was dimly aware of this mess but was reluctant to do anything about it, as the matriarch of the St. Goofy's family was something of a force in the community. The enterprising business manager and the interim pastor uncovered two new facts: the land St. Goofy's building was on had become valuable due to development in the area, and the matriarch was using the church service as a way to maintain power in her highly dysfunctional family. It was clear that St. Fungo's was not doing any ministry at St. Goofy's and that the asset was being squandered.

The interim pastor, who had no history with either the congregation or the matriarch, met with the remaining family, gave them a deadline for closing St. Goofy's, and offered St. Fungo's as a place where they could continue to worship. Not surprisingly, the matriarch turned down the offer and the quasi-congregation went elsewhere. The land and the building were subsequently sold and the proceeds placed in a special fund for ministry to people "on the other side of the tracks."

If your church has a program, staff position, land, or real estate that does not contribute to the core values and purpose, the interim period is a good time to make a change. The role of interim pastor includes taking out the garbage for a congregation. Nobody wants to take out the garbage, but everyone is grateful that someone does!

Turning Anger into Garbage

Pastor Bottomley was a charismatic, popular leader who attracted many new members to his congregation over five years. He was wonderful with the children, always remembering their names and who their parents were. He preached inspiring sermons and visited those who needed visits. Unfortunately, he couldn't keep his hands off of the money. He began by adding 10 percent to his car mileage every month. After a couple of years he was recording a good many bogus trips and other expenses, and he found a way to intercept cash contributions.

Eventually a new auditor who was not a member of the parish looked closely at the pastor's expense accounts and thought that they looked suspiciously like personal expenses rather than professional expenses. Digging deeper, the auditor checked the mileage reports, calling members who lived more that fifteen miles from the church to see if they really had five visits from Pastor Bottomley in one month. The auditor subsequently blew the whistle on Bottomley, who denied everything. When the Board became involved, word of the pastor's difficulties began to leak to the congregation and people began to take sides. The judicatory became involved and checked the work of the auditor. The pastor was given the ultimatum to resign or face criminal charges. He left, but only after setting fire to the parish hall.

Needless to say, Pastor Bottomley did not have many friends left in the parish by the time he went over the horizon. The parishioners were hurt and outraged. The trained interim pastor who took over was greeted with suspicion just for being a pastor. In time she managed to help the parishioners to vent their anger. She encouraged people to wrap up their anger in a metaphorical trash bag and drop it in front of the altar. While the departure of Pastor Bottomley helped relieve a lot of the anger, the work of the interim pastor was critical in helping this congregation prepare to call a new pastor.

As Philip said in *Ten Dumb Things Churches Do*, sometimes the dumb thing is the pastor. Whatever he or she did may have infuriated you. If you're still mad, what are you going to do with that anger now that the pastor is gone? Consider St. Paul's advice: "Put away from you all bitterness and wrath and anger and wrangling and slander, together with all malice, and be kind to one another, tenderhearted, forgiving one another, as God in Christ has forgiven you." (Ephesians 4:31–32)

Easier said than done. Forgiveness is hard. Philip tells this story from his own experience:

> Some years ago I went into a business partnership with a man with whom I was acquainted but did not know well on a personal level. The business venture was a restaurant, and like 90 percent of all restaurants, it failed. We both lost a lot of money. We both blamed each other. We were both responsible for the errors that led to the failure.
>
> The reason I knew this guy was that we attended the same church, which we continued to do after the business failure. My attendance was sporadic because I was doing supply preaching much of the time and his attendance was sporadic because he traveled a good deal. I do not recall our paths crossing for the entire year after the business failure. The first time we were both at the same service, it was the Easter Vigil. We ended up seated more or less across the aisle from each other. I remember that for the first half of the service

my thoughts were primarily about what I was going to do at the time of passing of the peace. I really wanted to reconcile, but I was afraid of his response. We would have to meet in the middle of the center aisle. Whatever happened would be public.

Of course this was the Easter Vigil, with the nine lessons, the hymns, and the lighting of the Paschal candle all focused on God's ultimate act of reconciliation. I sensed that it was time to reconcile. I think we both knew it. At the words, "The peace of the Lord be always with you," we both headed to the aisle and exchanged the Peace of Christ with each other and really meant it. I'm proud of the fact that we did it. I'm not proud of the fact that it took a year to do it.

When the departing pastor leaves behind a heap of anger, there is not much opportunity for reconciliation as there was for Philip and his business partner. Yet while you may be unable to reconcile with the offensive pastor, you *can* reconcile within yourself the pain and disappointment you have experienced. Time will make things better *if* you permit love to replace the hurt. Children know how to do this: when they are hurt, they seek a parent, for they feel better in the arms of the parent. The angry parishioner must seek the Heavenly Parent in the same way. From the safety of God's arms you may be able to forgive the wayward pastor. Our sinful anger begins to dissipate when we can pray, "Forgive us our sins as we forgive those who sin against us," and really mean it.

So work to discard the anger—throw it out with the garbage.

Keeping the Trains Running

This is a very short section. That is not to suggest that keeping things going in a parish during the interim time is always easy, but in reality, most churches have enough momentum to keep going for some time after a pastor leaves, even without an interim pastor. In some churches, lay leadership steps up and becomes stronger in the absence of a pastor. It can be a revelation for a congregation to discover that the walls don't crumble because the pastor leaves, in other words, to realize that the pastor is not God. But a church without pastoral leadership will not flourish indefinitely. If the congregation becomes paralyzed and unable to make decisions about anything, members may begin to drift off. Attendance and income will drop and the situation begins to lose focus.

An interim pastor can inject some new ideas into the system to keep things fresh and vital. The interim pastor may detect that one of the trains she has been asked to keep running is, in fact, off the track. For example, St. Wilhelmina's rang a set of Sanctus bells at the appropriate moment in the communion service, even though the practice was jarringly inconsistent with the otherwise simple celebration of the Holy Eucharist. It turned out that the Sanctus bells had been a memorial gift. A previous pastor had tried to discontinue their use, but caved when he learned the reason the bells were inserted in the liturgy in the first place.

An interim pastor can keep the trains running, but it may not always be the best thing to keep them running exactly as they were. If one of the trains is off the track, it may be time relegate it to the maintenance shed. It will be beneficial to the parish and the new pastor at least to raise a few questions about *why* things are done the way they are and to gently and lovingly teach some different ways of doing things based on adherence to the core values of the church.

Preparing for the New Pastor

Preparing for the new pastor is every bit as important as coping with the past and keeping the ministry going. A good interim pastor can get the congregation ready for the transition to the new pastor by doing a number of things.

1. **Identity Check.**
   The newest person in an organization is usually the person best able to see its values and processes clearly. As a "professional newcomer," the trained interim pastor can help a congregation learn something about who they are, so that they will be better able to call the right person to be their pastor. While the standard practice of having the search committee conduct a survey is helpful, there is a potential weakness in the process. Questionnaires that are written and analyzed by members of the

parish inevitably incorporate the congregation's blind spots, causing important information to be missed. The congregation may also overlook unusual gifts and talents it has because these are assumed to be a normal part of any church community. The Interim Pastor should hold up a mirror to the parish through preaching and teaching so that the parish can embrace its special gifts and seek to amend things that need to be changed. With a measure of grace dropped by the Holy Spirit, the congregation may see the necessity of changing qualities that may interfere with their response to God's call to step into the future.

2. **Change Something in Worship.**

   Even if an interim pastor is determined not to make changes in the worship life of a congregation, it is inevitable that he or she will not do the liturgy exactly as the recently retired Pastor Goodbody did. Such variations as the clergy's personality and his or her special abilities in drama or music inevitably produce differences in the liturgy. So even if the interim wishes to simply keep the liturgy train running as it was, the simple fact of her or his leadership in the service makes it different. Given that fact, the interim pastor will do the next pastor a big favor by intentionally exposing the congregation to some new possibilities in their worship life. New hymns, prayers, and whole liturgies are out there in the wider church, and the new pastor will certainly bring some new material. Preparing the congregation to get over the mantra, "We always did it this way," is an important part of the interim period.

3. **Getting the Structure Right.**

   The interim period is a good time to make changes in the organizational scheme if the church has the wrong one for its size. The most common problem is the program size church that is still operating as a pastoral size church. The trained interim pastor should be able to spot this kind of mismatch and take steps to correct it.

   Bear in mind that in the case of the pastoral-to-program size growth progression, one can change the structure but the culture will lag behind. It will take a while to train the congregation to understand that the pastor will not know everyone and will not know all of the details of every program. On the other hand, the church board can be trained fairly quickly to adopt the program church model of board members serving as liaisons to committees. This replaces the model of the board and the pastor micromanaging every aspect of parish life.

A church may need to revise its organizational scheme because of expansion from program size to resource size, or of contraction from program size to pastoral size. In any case that requires structural reorganization, the interim pastor should start on this transition as early as possible in order to have the appropriate organizational model working before the new pastor arrives. The search committee also needs to understand that they are seeking a pastor with experience in the size church the parish is moving towards, not the size they are leaving behind.

See Chapter 5, which is all about this topic.

4. **Communications Check.**

The interim period is a good time to address the state of the church's communications. While the interim period is not necessarily the time to develop a whole new look and feel for all publications and the Web site, it is a good time to look at how communication flows from the parishioners, committees, and staff to the service bulletins, verbal announcements, and monthly newsletter. Is there too much information or not enough? Would a different format for the service sheet be more "green" or more user-friendly? Is the Web site being refreshed often? Attention to the Web site is especially important because for a church in the search process pastoral candidates will be looking there to find out who you are. Having pictures of the parish picnic from two years ago does not speak well for your congregation!

See Chapter 9, which is all about this topic.

Tips for the Search Process

Before departing the realm of interim ministry, here are a few tips for the search process:

1. All search committee members should agree in writing to the following:

   - We understand that this process is very time consuming.
   - We will do our best to be objective in our evaluations of our work.
   - We will openly communicate our ideas to other church leaders.
   - We will regularly communicate our progress to the congregation.
   - We will be a team.
   - We will respect confidentiality.
   - We will support the directives of the parish profile.
   - We will pray regularly for a successful search.

2. The search committee should do team building to get to know each other well before they start evaluating applicants. Taking time in the beginning to understand one another's core values will save the committee time in the long run.

3. Make certain that the search committee does not burn out before they finish the job. If your church is large enough, break out the search team responsibilities into separate task groups. Appoint a team to do the research necessary to generate your profile and another team of skilled writers to write the profile. Then give the finished profile to the search team and turn them loose.

4. If your judicatory has the ability to prescreen candidates, engage their help to eliminate the task of wading through hundreds of pages of résumés, cover letters, old sermons, etc.

5. If your church is healthy, consider shrinking the interim time by starting the search process while the departing pastor is still on board. This will work best if the departing pastor is retiring.

6. Visit other churches in your area. Find out what the competition is doing.

7. Remember, the perfect pastor does not exist.

Hospitality:
Welcoming the Newcomer and Other Strangers

But now in Christ Jesus you who once were far off have been brought near by the blood of Christ. For he is our peace; in his flesh he has made both groups into one and has broken down the dividing wall, that is, the hostility between us.

—Ephesians 2:13–14

Breaking Down the Walls

A man recounted the story of his first visit to the church where he is now a member. That Sunday morning he entered the sanctuary, accepted a bulletin from an usher, and took a seat at the end of a pew near the back of the church. As he sat listening to the prelude, an elderly lady came up the aisle and stopped a few feet from him. She glared pointedly at the newcomer until he received the unspoken message, "You are sitting in my pew," and hastily moved back a row. Despite that inauspicious beginning, he subsequently joined the church, whose mission statement declares them to be "welcoming."

In the letter to the Ephesians we read that Christ is breaking down the dividing walls of hostility between people and creating a united humanity, "built upon the foundation of the apostles and prophets, with Christ Jesus himself as the cornerstone. In him the whole structure is joined together and grows into a holy temple in the Lord; in whom you also are built together spiritually into a dwelling place for God" (Ephesians 2:20–22). This image of the estranged human family being remade into a temple where God dwells speaks to our deepest inner longings. We want to experience in the church a foretaste of that peaceful world in which walls enclose rather than separate us.

As members of Christ's body, we recognize that we are supposed to offer radical hospitality in his name, and a church's stated values may be clear about our responsibility to welcome the stranger. Our *operational* values (i.e., what we actually do), on the other hand, are often something else. We might talk about welcoming the stranger, but we operate along the lines of the sentiment expressed by a wary New England farmer in Robert Frost's poem *Mending Wall*: "Good fences make good neighbors." Sometimes the divider we make is a space rather than a wall, as demonstrated by churches that split apart for all kinds of reasons. The fact is, we're more comfortable with dividing walls and gaps than we are with the friction of rubbing up against other people.

Even our language keeps us apart. Think how often in conversation we refer to others as "those people" or "they." "*Those people* come over to our country and expect _____," or, "*They* just don't appreciate hard work." "They" are the strangers in our midst, people from other countries, with different accents, different customs of religion and food, different ways of being family. Whoever "they" are, they are different from us, and we are wary of them.

We keep making barriers Jesus never imposed. When he fed the five thousand, the Gospel accounts (Matthew 14:13–21, Luke 9:10–17) do not mention that there was any identity check prior to the distribution of the loaves and fishes. Certainly that vast crowd must have included Jews of various sects, Gentiles of many ethnicities, people of every age and social status. The radical inclusiveness that Jesus practiced is a stated belief of our faith that turns up again and again in church profiles in words such as: "We are a welcoming Christian community." But rarely is it an operational belief in our congregations. How can we genuinely change the corporate culture in such a way as to welcome the stranger as well as to honor the stranger for who she is and what she brings to the community? Is this radical change even possible?

In 1996, Hurricane Fran created havoc when it ripped through Raleigh. The rear of our house was crushed by an enormous tree that stove in the roof and practically cut off the kitchen. Before we could begin reconstruction, there was some demolition to do. Phil remembers taking a crowbar and sledgehammer and flailing away at the old wall for an entire day. "By the end of the day, I was exhausted and ached all over. Worst of all, I had not actually done much; there was still a lot left to do the next day. Our contractor said not to worry because the shovel on the payloader would take care of it. In fact it took about ten minutes for the heavy equipment to complete the demolition that would have required at least two more days of my time. It was a relief, but in a way, it just wasn't as satisfying as the physical labor. Tearing down something can be fun."

Moving the church's invisible walls can be every bit as tough as dismantling actual walls. Sometimes even small changes like introducing new hymns or changing the carpet in the sanctuary meet with major resistance from a congregation that wants things to just stay comfortable and familiar. It probably isn't realistic to think that such a church can suddenly change its corporate culture and become warm and welcoming.

Perhaps, though, we can learn to move those walls a little bit each time a newcomer comes to our community. It is not enough just to welcome the stranger with a handshake and invite them to the coffee hour. When we ask questions of newcomers, we need to listen carefully to their answers, not merely to find out what committee they could serve on but more importantly, to determine how *we* can serve *them*.

In one church the newcomers committee courted a new young couple in the hope that they would come to see that the parish was right for them. To their credit, the committee understood that engaging the couple in the life of the congregation was an important step. Unfortunately, however, they made the mistake of asking the newcomers to serve on the cemetery committee. The couple took this as an ill omen and did not return. We need to listen and learn where people are on their faith journeys, not just plug them into an inquirer's class or burden them with our issues. We need to honor people for who they are, as Jesus taught and did.

The defining "walls" of our corporate culture need to be flexible enough to permit newcomers to enter. Of course, there are limits. If the seeker wants to discover how animal sacrifice at your altar can improve his or her spiritual life, you may have to make it clear that your corporate cultural wall is not infinitely expandable. Each congregation will have to define the limits of their stated beliefs (that we hope are also their operational beliefs). Also, we need to recognize that when we move a wall out in one direction, we may pull the wall in on the opposite side.

When the Episcopal Church approved same-sex unions and the ordination of gays and lesbians, many conservative Episcopalians perceived that the boundaries of the church had shifted in a way that left them out. Although church leaders emphasized that even vigorous anti-gay folk were still included in the denomination, not everyone felt that was true. At this point the actual beliefs of some members no longer fell within the stated beliefs of the denomination. Parishes are still coping with this particular mismatch of stated, personal, and operational beliefs.

Strength in Diversity

Here is where the problem of genuine diversity can smack us around. It takes time for us to develop truly inclusive hearts. We know that Jesus' association with women, tax collectors, lepers, and others whom society did not value was at first distressing to his disciples. Again and again in his interactions with people, he points to their intrinsic worth as human beings and uses the overturning of certain norms as "teachable moments." The change of heart didn't happen all at once, but in time the disciples became flexible enough to expand and nurture the church in a hostile environment.

Just as the disciples' experience of the Crucifixion and Resurrection played a part in their change of heart, any radical transformation that takes place in us must be energized by the same basic paradigm of our faith: **life → death → new life**. Whenever we invite the stranger into our midst and take the time to learn who he or she is, some old prejudice in us dies, some old wall falls, and we discover the humanity in the stranger we initially dreaded.

Parents of gay and lesbian children are a good example of this kind of change. When parents learn that their children are homosexual, their first response may range from disappointment to outright revulsion. But for many parents, as they discover their child's happiness in the presence of the gay or lesbian partner, old prejudices die and new life takes hold. While this does not always happen, it has happened often enough that we draw encouragement from it. This emerging pattern should embolden us to risk facing down our prejudices to meet other strangers on a human level.

The Church as Home

Ephesians describes the church as nothing less than a home for God. At its best, the church is also a home for our spirits, a place that helps us experience for a little while life as it might be for the entire family of humanity.

The word "home" carries lots of emotional associations for most of us. Homelessness is regarded as one of the worst tragedies that can befall a person in our society. If you are lucky enough to live in a home you love, you are blessed. We, the authors, have moved so many times that the U. S. Postal Service has trouble keeping track of our whereabouts (although curiously, our alumni magazines always seem to find us). So while we long to call a single place "home," our peripatetic life has not often offered us that opportunity. Our many changes of address have taught us one thing, though: home is not a building. We have learned that for each of us, home is where the other is, and when it's under the same roof, it's a good thing.

That's true of our church home, too. It's not a place; it's a state of being. Whether a congregation meets in an historic stone edifice, a storefront, or somebody's living room, they should aspire to be a home for God and a place where people feel truly at home.

These are three qualities of the church home:

1. **Home is a place where love abides**. Robert Frost wrote, "Home is the place where, when you have to go there, they have to take you in." Your church home is the place where the church family loves you and accepts you as you are, no matter what you did

last week or last year or ten years ago. The church home is a place where Christian love abides, following Jesus' simple but difficult commandment to love one another. That means that even when we fight, we hang in there with each other instead of stomping out of the building and going to find another church. In the church, as in a family, blood is thicker than water. The common humanity we share through the blood of Christ is more important, more binding, than petty squabbles that we have among ourselves.

2. A church home welcomes not only the church family—**it welcomes the stranger**. In fact, if a church practices Jesus' brand of radical hospitality, the needs of family may at times be displaced by those of the stranger. Newcomers give various reasons for attending a church for the first time, but mostly they are like the long-time members—they just want to be loved. It is important that they be fed by the worship life and Christian formation program and feel that they are genuinely welcomed and accepted for who they are—not merely as a new pledge unit or volunteer for the Sunday School.

   A desire to truly welcome the stranger creates a dilemma for the church: is it more important to make the worship and programs of our church comfortable for ourselves or to make them welcoming for the stranger? Or do we believe those are the same things? Most of us think of our home parish as a welcoming church. But we also want our church to be the way *we* want it, to feed us the way *we* like to be nourished. When we come home, we want home to be familiar, not to find that our parents rented out our room in our absence. (Linda remembers once coming home from college to discover that her room had been taken over by her younger brother who had decorated the ceiling with dozens of sets of shark jaws that gaped menacingly in the night!) Nevertheless, some changes in our homes happen for good reasons, and the church is no different. Pastors and staff come and go. Members come and go. The building is expanded or remodeled. The neighborhood changes. Can the church be home for us *and* for the stranger?

Paul says that the greatest of the three things that endure in this transient world is love. Church is the place where you are loved no matter what. You may be asked to give up your favorite seat to a stranger, but you are loved and you are called to love the stranger.

3. **Everyone is baptized in the same Living Water.** This is the thing that makes the long-time member and the stranger indistinguishable from one other. In baptism, those persistent differences that cause us to insist on the safety of walls and gaps are melted down. We emerge from the primordial womb of baptismal waters re-formed, ready to live a new kind of life offered in the household of Christ. The water makes it possible for every one of us to come home again and again, just as we are.

At its best, the church is our true home, that paradoxical place where people are accepted, warts and all, and where at the same time they are freed and empowered to discover the best that is in them.

Bringing an Outsider In

To make our churches radically inclusive, we have to be willing to move the walls. This story captures something of what the Good News is all about.

> During the Second World War there lived in a small village in Poland a man who was known for his compassion for others. He was not a particularly wealthy man and he was not a native of the village. In that Catholic country, he did not attend the village church, and he wasn't even baptized. But in his adopted village he was known for his good works. If a stranger came to the village and needed a place to stay, the man would offer a cot in his little home. If a family ran out of food, he was the first to offer a loaf of bread or some flour from his meager supplies. If someone was in trouble with the authorities or if the Germans, or later, the Russians, swept through the village to collect the young men for imprisonment or forced military service, he would help hide the victims in the woods. On account of all these things, he was greatly loved by the villagers.

It happened that this beloved man died. The villagers asked the priest to bury the man in the church cemetery. The priest, who knew and loved the man as much as the rest of the villagers did, agreed to conduct the funeral service. But he could not agree to the burial. He said, "I cannot bury him in our cemetery. It is hallowed ground. We must put him where the unbaptized are buried. Those are the rules of the church and I cannot change them."

The villagers protested that this good man was surely loved by God as much as any of the baptized, perhaps even more, because of all the good that he had done. The priest agreed that the man was virtuous, but insisted that the rules of the church could be not be broken. Finally he came up with a compromise that he hoped would satisfy everyone. He said, "I will bury him on church land, but it will have to be outside the fence that surrounds our cemetery."

And so a grave was prepared just outside the fence, and on the appointed day the villagers carried the beloved man's body in procession to the site. The priest conducted the service, then the grave was filled in, a stone was placed, and everyone went home.

But the next morning when the priest went to the church to conduct mass, he saw that something had happened during the night. The wall around the cemetery had been moved. Now the enclosure around the cemetery included the grave of the beloved man.[11]

As the villagers expanded the fence that enclosed hallowed ground to include the grave of the man they loved, so Jesus expanded the boundaries of humanity to such a degree that we are even commanded to love our enemies.

Enlarging the Perimeter

How can we make inclusiveness a reality in our churches? There is no simple checklist for this task, but here are a few things you can try:

- Take an "outsider's eye" view of your church by asking yourselves who doesn't feel welcome in your services. If your worship schedule excludes people who work on Sunday, for example, try offering a service at a nontraditional time such as Saturday evening. If your worshipers like to dress up on Sunday morning, you could offer a "come as you are" service that invites people to dress more informally.

- Make your building's handicapped accessibility clear in all your advertising: church signboard, Yellow Pages, Web site, and print ads.

- Offer newcomers an instructional class that includes the stated beliefs of the congregation. Give them time and safety to discuss their personal beliefs and reassure them that they will not be dismissed for their personal beliefs (unless they insist on practicing animal sacrifice in the chapel).

- Teach stewardship as part of the newcomers class and have participants fill out a pledge card along with the membership documents.

- Publicly recognize new members once they have passed through the instructional class and made a decision to join the church. Write short biographies with photos for the newsletter and Web site.

- Children of newcomers should also have opportunities to find out what is expected of them. Help them feel included with some kind of special welcoming ritual in Sunday School along with putting their pictures on the Web site. Note that your congregation's policy about posting photos on the Web site should take parents' wishes into consideration. Some parents will object to having their child's image posted in the public domain.

Remember that the goal is not only to welcome but also to affirm and accept.

-9-

Communications:
Show and Tell It on the Mountain

Now those who were scattered went from place to place, proclaiming the word.
—Acts 8:4

For many centuries churches were built in the middle of towns, right on the square, the plaza, or the green. The town square functioned as a public marketplace where farmers and crafters sold their goods and produce. That space also served as the communications hub, where people coming to market found out what was going on in the town and perhaps the neighboring towns. Larger churches and cathedrals even served as market places in bad weather well into the thirteenth and fourteenth centuries. Even livestock might be bought and sold on the floor of the nave.

Today our churches are built in all kinds of locations, and they no longer serve as gathering places for the whole community. So today we in the church have to be more deliberate about telling others who we are and perhaps even *where* we are. The shopping mall that replaced the town square in the second half of the twentieth century is itself now being replaced by the World Wide Web. Increasingly, the Web is where people prefer to go not only for shopping but also for information of all kinds. Likewise, e-mail is replacing postal mail, and text messaging is replacing short phone calls.

When we consider changes in the church's environment, communications technology is perhaps the most far-reaching area of change.

In this chapter we want to look at some aspects of communication that are of particular concern to churches. We seldom encounter a parish that is completely satisfied with their communications. Practically every church, large and small, would like to do a better job of communicating, whether that means producing an error-free weekly service bulletin, sharing information about decisions made by boards and committees, creating a dynamic Web site, or advertising church activities to the wider community.

The realm of communication is broader and deeper than we can begin to explore in this brief chapter. Our aim here is to give you a few pointers that may help improve your church's communications.

Internal Communications: Who Needs to Know?

There are many ways of talking about the things that make a church "go." Speaking theologically, we sometimes say that the Body of Christ is an entity sustained and empowered by the Holy Spirit. Or we may say that the church's life is fueled by passion or by mission. But it is also true to say that *the church runs on information.* The vitality of a church's life and ministry is closely connected with how effectively information is shared. The words "communication," "community," and "communion" all come from the Latin word *communicare*, meaning "to share." A healthy church community has good communications—good sharing of information.

In a church with good communications, vital information circulates freely, regularly reaching the appropriate persons through clearly established channels. In a church with good communications, members usually know what's going on, and anyone who doesn't knows where to go to find out. A church with good communications does *not* routinely have people caught unaware because somebody forgot to tell the church secretary that an event was cancelled or rescheduled. If people don't know what's going on and committee meetings are followed by long discussions in the parking lot or clandestine phone calls to certain church members, there is likely something amiss with communications. That being said, even in a church that holds a special meeting to vote on whether Jesus Christ really was the son of God and announces the meeting in the monthly newsletter, several weekly bulletins, and verbal announcements during the worship services, there will always be someone who says, "What special meeting?"

The church council of the Church in-the-Dark-Forest, a program size congregation, were wringing their hands over the "problem" of their communications. Council members felt that the congregation just didn't know what was going on enough of the time. Since the council members served as liaisons to the boards and committees of the church, there was a simple solution. The new interim pastor suggested that each time the council made a decision, they pause to ask the question, "Who else needs to know this?" In most instances this would mean the parish secretary, as the point person for communication; the newsletter editor; and any boards or committees affected. If a planned event required the use of the nursery, the childcare team needed to be alerted. If an event would be of interest to the community, the local newspaper should be included. The result was that with the addition of a communications stream to the decision process, the congregation soon began to feel much better about their parish life.

Communications and Church Size

Have you had occasion to call a telecommunications company lately? We have learned that when one of us wants to talk to customer service at one of these behemoths, it is best to start out the process in a calm and positive frame of mind with plenty of open time—perhaps a couple of hours—a good book, and a pleasant beverage. We know that the call will be an adventure in negotiating a complicated phone tree with multiple options, being transferred from one rep to another, explaining our request and customer number numerous times, being placed on hold to listen to music or to commercials, and often not resolving the issue we set out to deal with. The irony of a communications company that fails to communicate well with its customers is hard to miss.

Most churches are not of such a size that a caller has to go through a complicated phone tree to make an appointment to see the pastor. Nevertheless, in any church we can create Byzantine paths of communication by a failure to take up problems directly with the person involved. Telling the pastor's spouse about a problem the pastor should address makes for triangular communication that can be every bit as frustrating and distorted as trying to explain to the customer service rep that your cable television is not receiving the movie you just ordered. (The fact that the customer service rep is located on one of the outer rings of Saturn may add to the communications problem.) We have some wonderful technology at our command, but communicating well always comes down to one person having the ability to say or write what he or she really means in a way that someone else can understand it. The church is in the communications business in its own way, so there are really no excuses for not paying close attention to communications, no matter how big or small your church may be.

The mechanics of internal parish communications depend to some extent on the size of the church and how the pastor or lay leaders function in the system. In a pastoral-sized church, where members expect to have one-on-one access to the pastor, people are likely to depend on the pastor, the parish secretary, newsletter and bulletin announcements, and word of mouth to keep them in the know about what's going on. Most clergy know that members frequently share important information with the pastor in passing on Sunday morning and expect (unrealistically) him or her to follow up with a pastoral call or an appropriate announcement. Very few clergy are able to remember all the important information that may be imparted in conversation. Effective communication, not to mention the pastor's sanity, depends on his or her breaking the members of this practice!

The effectiveness of communications in a church that relies on the pastor and secretary to spread information depends largely on their talents. Pastors in some smaller churches routinely meet with all the boards and committees, share important information with these groups, and remember to inform the secretary of important announcements. That system works fine for some churches. On the other hand, a more introverted pastor who does not relish acting as the parish communicator may leave it to the secretary and lay leaders to get things announced. In a pastoral or family size church, perhaps the single most effective thing that can happen to improve communications is repeatedly to pose the question, "Who else needs to know this?" and *make sure someone follows up.*

At the other end of the size spectrum, larger membership churches (resource or large program) often have sufficient resources to employ staff members with responsibility for communications. Their roles may include a range of functions including production of internal publications such as worship bulletins, newsletters, and special documents like Lenten booklets; managing a Web site; coordinating public relations; and producing broadcasts. Even churches with such a wealth of resources need to pay attention to the internal flow of essential information. The question, "Who else needs to know this?" applies to them, too.

Some years ago the rector of a large resource size church adopted an ingenious practice to help with internal communications. Each Sunday as he greeted several hundred worshipers at the end of the service, his secretary would stand beside him with pen and notepad at the ready. Her function was to capture all the valuable information that parishioners shared with the rector on their way out the door. It was a system that worked brilliantly to help him keep up with pastoral needs.

Internal communications can be particularly vexing for program-sized churches. Their membership is usually too large for the kind of direct member-to-pastor contact enjoyed by smaller congregations with a single pastor. And while they may be able to employ more than one staff person, they probably don't have the resources to employ a parish communicator. Unless someone is paying attention to communication, information may fall through the cracks and members may think to themselves, "I used to know everyone and we used to be one big family, but now I don't know what's going on half the time." We believe that weakness of internal communications may be a contributing factor in the instability that causes some churches to grow to program size, then fall back to pastoral size.

In a program size church, therefore, it is especially important to establish clear decision pathways and communications channels. The church may well already have in place avenues for effective communication through newsletters, bulletins, announcements, phone trees, e-mail, and a Web site. The critical factor is for someone—a communications task group or a designated individual—to *pay attention to information flow* and to make sure gaps and blockages are attended to promptly. Someone needs to keep asking that question, "Who else needs to know this?" and make sure the information keeps moving in the right directions.

In this era of instant communications delivered by sophisticated technologies, churches often feel that they are fighting a losing battle to keep up with information technology. Yet the use of complex technologies does not guarantee that we are communicating more effectively. Ironically, the weak link in our communications is often not inept use of technology but simple human error: nobody thought to tell the parish secretary that the time of the annual meeting had been changed, so the word didn't get out.

Into All the World: A Community of Communicators

Can you imagine your church without Bibles, hymnals or prayer books? How about the telephone, the computer, or photocopier? Contemporary church life is inconceivable without many communications media we take for granted, yet obviously none of these existed in the time of Jesus. From its very beginnings, the church has taken advantage of available technologies to share the Gospel with other people and to carry out the life and work of the church.

In our time, when more communications technologies exist than at any time in human history, the church has fantastic new opportunities. Perhaps the beginning of this new millennium is a time we are being called to broaden our understanding of stewardship beyond the time-honored rubric of "time, talent, and treasure" to include stewardship of Creation and of technology. Being good stewards of the earth and its resources includes responsibility to use the tools of communication in the best possible way.

External Communications: Getting the Word Out

Living in a communications-media saturated age, many of us have pet theories about communication in the church. For example, we like to think that our church would instantly have better communications if the parish just had more state-of-the-art equipment. Or we think that if only our pastor's inspiring messages could be broadcast on the airwaves, new worshipers by the thousands would crowd our sanctuaries.

Not necessarily. It is true that your church's communications *may* be improved in some areas by spending the bucks for better technology. Updating the sound system and acquiring a couple of good quality wireless microphones is an example of money well spent for many a church. But good communication is not fundamentally a matter of money. For goodness sake, don't make the mistake of starting your discussion of communications by looking at how much money you have, deciding you can't afford to communicate, and chucking the whole idea. Far more important than money is 1) thinking strategically about your communications and 2) paying attention to the details.

Thinking Strategically

There's a simple question that helps set you on the road to effective communications strategy: Who says what to whom using which media?

- **Who** is no mystery—it's your church.

Your answers to the other parts of the question will tell you the rest of what you need to know to communicate effectively.

- With **whom** outside the church do you wish to communicate? In other words, **who is your audience**? Please don't assume you already know the answer so you can skip this step! Taking time to define clearly the audience(s) you wish to reach helps you hone the message you want to send and determine the best media for sending it. For example, do you want to reach *new residents in your community*? That audience suggests certain strategies for both the content of your message and the ways you deliver it. Targeting new residents without a church affiliation calls for a different approach than informing the whole town, including members of other faith communities, about some exciting mission project your church is doing. How you answer the question of audience will determine how you go about communicating with them.

- **What** do you want to say? Do you want to let everyone in the town of West Elbow know what time your services are or that you have a certain style of worship or that you offer services in Spanish? Do you want to convey your congregation's conviction that Jesus is Lord and invite others to come to your church to talk about that? Once you put together the content of your message, take time to focus and polish it carefully before you distribute it. Poor grammar or sloppy graphics can send the unintended message that you don't know any better—or don't care.

- **Using which media?** Choosing the particular media you will use to reach your intended audience isn't just a question of the technologies available to you, and it isn't just about how much you can afford to spend. It's partly a question about how the audience you wish to reach prefers to get its information. All of us are bombarded daily with far more information than we can possibly use, and quite reasonably, we are increasingly selective about how we capture the information we really want. So your church shouldn't rely on a single medium of communication. You can use the good old church sign to announce the times of your worship services. But you should also use your knowledge of your community to share information via such means as announcements in the local paper, ads in the phone book, and fliers on bulletin boards in places your potential worshipers hang out. Perhaps the most important thing you can do is to have a dynamic, up-to-date Web site. Different audiences and different messages require different media.

You get the idea. It's essential to know what you want to say and to which audiences you want to say it. Once you figure that out, you can get on with deciding which of many options you want to use for getting your message out.

Geeks, Technophobes, and Luddites

The reality that many churches have aging memberships is not news. A 2008 survey published by the Pew Forum on Religion and Public Life indicates that more than half of mainline Protestants in the U.S.

are fifty or older. We discussed in an earlier chapter how some of the differences between older and younger generations in American society are expressed in our churches.

One of the clearest distinctions between generations is how people of different ages prefer to get their information. Those of us (including the authors) old enough to be grandparents grew up in a print-dominated world. Books were the basis of our education and newspapers the principal source of our knowledge of world events, while television and non-print media were primarily for entertainment. But for our children and grandchildren, the Information Age presents a whole different ball game. Computers and electronic media are their birthright. Young people e-mail, they text message, they post details of their lives on MySpace. Of course, young people still learn their ABCs and read novels, and many grandparents happily use computers, but there is a sense in which the separate generations are citizens of different cultures.

So churches are in an interesting situation. The "graying" American church, as indicated by the Pew survey, retains a bias toward print. Print technologies dominate church life in the form of Bibles, hymnals, prayer books, printed service sheets, mailing lists, and newsletters. And because this is how church has always been for the majority of church members, it's hard to get many age fifty-five-plus church members to see that print is now *one among many* ways to facilitate worship and share our faith. In a way, generational bias blinds older Americans to the possibility of using new technologies in the church. Many adult church members who employ an array of technologies in their work life find parish life to be a time warp, where the parish secretary still uses a Selectric typewriter and the treasurer keeps financial records in an old-fashioned hardback ledger. As for our Web-surfing, texting, video game-playing children, coming to church is like visiting a museum.

The church's schizoid attitude toward old and new technologies is reflected in many aspects of parish life. If you circulate through the parish hall during the coffee hour, for example, you are equally likely to witness someone whipping out a PDA to make a note of a lunch date or hear, "What's your e-mail address?" as you are to hear boasts like, "I don't have a computer. I don't even have an answering machine!"

We are not, of course, advocating the use of technology for its own sake. We are saying that it is important to realistically assess how members of your church prefer to get their information, and more importantly, how the people you want to attract prefer to get their information, and to act accordingly. Many of the church search profiles we read state that the church wants to attract younger members. It is doubtful that you will be able to do that if your communications remain wedded to nineteenth-century technologies.

Change is hard. We don't want to change things too much because we don't want to alienate the members. Ironically, some of the things churches cherish most dearly today started out by upsetting people quite a lot. When the Book of Common Prayer was introduced by the Church of England in 1549, religious conservatives were incensed by its elimination of traditional Roman Catholic practices and introduction of Lutheran-influenced theology. Riots in such heavily Roman Catholic areas as Devon and Cornwall led to the crown's dispatch of armed troops. In the end, several thousands of protestors either died in the conflict or were executed. Major change can have drastic consequences.

The Web Site

It bears repeating that the single most important communications tool for any church is an attractive, up-to-date Web site. You may object that not all your members are on the Internet. That doesn't matter, because the Web site isn't primarily for your members—it's the virtual front door to your church, the face you present to the world. The Web is the marketplace and information hub for the world, and your church Web site is the number one way newcomers to the community shop for a church home. If your church is in a pastoral search, the Web site is probably the first place candidates will go to get information about your congregation. It's where others in your denomination go to find out about your programs and resources. Besides all that, it may also serve your membership as an electronic notice board, if you wish, with some pages accessible only to church members.

If you don't yet have a Web site, it's a good idea to check with your judicatory to see what resources they have. Most conference or diocesan offices have communications staff officers to advise you, and some denominations offer templates that make it easy to put up a Web site. They may even have the means to host your Web site at a reasonable cost. If you don't have denominational resources at hand, look within your congregation for Web-savvy talent who could help create a site for the church. It's also possible to hire someone to do it for a modest charge.

Regardless of how you create a Web site for your church, the most important thing is to *keep it current.* We have looked at hundreds of church Web sites, and they often leave us feeling sad. Why? Because they look abandoned. There are no people depicted, no activities mentioned, no signs of life. Almost as sad are sites where clicking on a calendar link brings up activities for September of last year, or a click on the photo gallery button produces images of the Easter egg hunt from 2004. What a different and happy experience it is to find a church Web site with abundant pictures of the life of the community, information about what church groups are doing this week, an up-to-date worship schedule, and other signs of life. A vibrant Web site makes a visitor say, "I'd like to know those people."

A Web site may be simple or it may be fancy, but to be worth anything at all, it has to be up to date. And that means someone needs to have responsibility for it.

Tips

Effective communication is *not* a function of how much money your church can throw at it. While it's nice to dream of having a dedicated staff position for communications or six figures' worth of new audio-visual equipment in the sanctuary, you can make major improvements in your communications that will cost you time and attention but not much money. Here are a few of them:

- Learn the Golden Rule of information so you can apply it to all planning, evaluation, and administrative functions within your church: always ask, "Who else needs to know this?" *and* always make sure somebody responsible is following up to pass the information through appropriate channels. Be sure to include an information stream in your planning, regardless of whether you use a simple checklist or a project management process. And following important events, by all means include communications in your evaluation process so you can keep improving.

- Create a consistent "look and feel" for your parish communications. If you don't have a logo, get someone to design one for you. Create a "tagline" or short phrase that identifies your church (e.g., "a traditional Christian community in the heart of West Elbow"). Include the logo and tagline on all your church communications, including bulletins, Web site, print ads, t-shirts, and anything else you generate. Adopting one type font to use in all your print materials also helps achieve a consistent look.

- Have a communications strategy, coherent communications policies, and designated communicators to execute them. For specific initiatives like launching a Web site, you can recruit a team of members with skills such as technical computer know-how, writing, and layout. There also needs to be one or more persons who will coordinate with the board and the parish secretary to ensure that information flows through internal channels and to check external communications for quality control (e.g., Is the Web site fresh? Does the sign advertising Easter services include the church logo?).

- People who are inundated with information (i.e., all of us) will thank you for prioritizing information for them. Use devices like **bold typefonts** or highlighted text or text boxes for important stuff. Summarize lengthy items with bullets. And put the most important information first.

- Designate an official photographer to document church events and provide abundant high-quality images for the Web site and publications. The photographer should be someone who is good with a digital camera and has some understanding of how his or her decisions in setting up photos will affect the appearance of photos on the Web. For example:

  - Set the camera for enough pixels per picture to allow for the size space it will occupy on the web page.

- Pictures of people eating rarely look good even though this is what many congregations spend a lot of time doing.
- Close ups of people are better than long shots.
- Pictures of more than one person should say something about the relationship of the people to each other and perhaps the activity—a parent holding a child, the youth group with their arms around each other in front of the soup kitchen they visited, etc.
- Posed pictures are good because people are generally looking at the camera. Pictures of this sort are inviting to visitors.
- A picture of an empty church makes a statement. Is it the one you want to make?

- The church secretary or administrator is key to effective communications. She or he should have proper tools to work with, including a computer that was manufactured in this century. Since a secretary may not welcome the learning curve that comes with new equipment, it may be a good investment to send him or her to a local course or professional training event especially for parish administrators.

- Cultivate a relationship with the religion reporter for the local newspaper. A reporter who knows your parish or is acquainted with your pastor is more likely to call you for a quote for a story or to turn a press release about an interesting mission project into an article.

- Go green. If you have a well-functioning Web site and send out weekly email updates to members, allow parishioners who prefer these electronic communications to opt out of hard-copy mailings. Once a significant number of folk are receiving church communications electronically, you may reach a point where the mailing list falls below the minimum number for bulk mailing. That's okay! A cost analysis sometimes shows that it is actually cheaper to print fewer newsletters and send them at the regular postal rate than to send hundreds of copies at bulk rate to an inflated mailing list.

Finally, evaluate. Find someone who is not a member of your parish to help you look at your communications objectively. You and the church members may think that your logo derived from the distinctive shape of your altar is a winner, but will it mean anything to someone visiting your Web site?

The Big Finish

We end this book where the first one started: the dumbest thing churches do is to operate out of fear rather than out of trust and love. This fear is manifested in folk most every time a church leader suggests that change may be necessary.

Almost a decade into the twenty-first century, there have been countless books devoted to the changes that we are already experiencing on our planet and will experience in the years ahead. The Body of Christ cannot afford to ignore change; we must adapt to or confront changes in our environment based on our core beliefs and values. And we must understand that the Body of Christ is a living organism and therefore, constantly changing. The love of God is the one unchanging reality, but we may have to learn how to express it in new ways. As we said in the Introduction, we are still under Jesus' command to Peter to "feed the sheep," but we need not be afraid to find new ways of doing so. This final chapter is a brief look at how we might go about this task.

❖10❖

Change:
The New Millennium Has Left the Station (and Won't Come Back for You)

We must be the change we wish to see in the world.
—Gandhi

Listen, I tell you a mystery: We will not all sleep, but we will all be changed.
—1 Corinthians 15:51 (NIV)

O ne church, in a playful spirit, framed these words from 1 Corinthians and hung them on the wall of the crib room. Of course, the change in question isn't really confined to diapers. Paul is telling us that believers will be completely transformed in the Kingdom of God. Most of us claim to welcome the idea that God will completely and utterly change us in the Hereafter. What bothers church members is immediate, tangible changes.

A successful executive addressing a sales meeting said:

Change has considerable psychological impact on the human mind. To the fearful it is threatening because it means that things may get worse. To the hopeful it is encouraging because things may get better. To the confident it is inspiring because the challenge exists to make things better. Obviously, then, one's character and frame of mind determine how readily he brings about change and how he reacts to change that is imposed on him.[12]

One reason that parishioners find it hard to cope with change is the feeling of powerlessness it evokes. Think about some of the factors that cause change. Some of them—aging, economic shifts, and natural disasters—we cannot control. Others can possibly be controlled if lots of people work together—global warming, for example. Certain other potential change-makers, such as marital status and how we earn a living, we can partially control. What we have the most control of is what we do from moment to moment. We may feel that our choices are limited, that we cannot really change what we do, but we can always choose to do nothing. To that degree we can control change. We can either embrace it or reject it. If we reject change, we may end up standing still while everyone goes elsewhere.

Some people embrace change by deliberately varying their breakfast menu. Others prefer to have the same breakfast every morning because it requires no thought at a time of day when one is slow and stupid. There is no right or wrong about the breakfast menu. However, in our churches people seldom voluntarily embrace the new and unfamiliar. Indeed, they often repel change, insisting on having "it" (whatever "it" is) the way we always had "it" because it gives us pleasure and comfort to have "it" that way. In a way it's like going to the same mountain cabin every summer: there is some comfort in the predictability. When you show up at church on Sunday, you want to have a fairly good idea of what is going to happen, i.e., predictability. But a church is not a bowl of breakfast cereal.

In our mainline churches today we are dealing constantly with tension elicited by change. A congregation may understand in a rational sense that change is necessary because such factors as demographics, music preferences, and our understanding of sexuality are changing; but the idea that the parish itself may require a major overhaul is usually too much for the folk to bear.

It's useful to distinguish between *reactive* change and *proactive* change. Reactive change is forced by a shift in the context, whereas proactive change anticipates a change in the context. The emerging church has done well by anticipating changes in the context and changing proactively. Mainline churches are too often responding to rapid contextual changes with glacial speed. We have written about some of these changes in previous chapters, especially in the area of communications.

Towards Something and Away from Something Else

Any congregation that has been around for at least ten years has some fairly set ways of doing things. Therefore they will have a difficult time embracing a proactive change, even when the people know perfectly well that they called the new minister with the idea that he or she would make some changes.

One congregation whose new building sat empty most weekdays wanted the new pastor to find some creative uses for the meeting rooms. A concern for good stewardship of their physical assets motivated them to try to either gain some rental income for use of the space or find a worthwhile program that would benefit from the use of space for free. The local homeless shelter approached the church regarding use of a room on cold weekdays during the winter. Their winter shelter program needed a place for elderly persons who did not have jobs to be during the day. The shelter's licensing did not permit them to operate the shelter facility both day and night.

The church had plenty of empty rooms, but the request was ultimately turned down. The reasons given were numerous: strangers walking about the halls would be a security risk, the stuff that was in the room would have to be moved elsewhere, etc. While these objections were clearly trivial to most observers, each one was critical to someone. The church increased its financial gift to the shelter and the manager went elsewhere to seek space.

The idea of doing something for the homeless shelter seemed a good idea, consistent with the mission of the church. The problem was that *it meant giving up something.* A church can more easily deal with a financial cost than other kinds of costs such as loss of control of time and space. For a change to take place, those involved must think through all of the consequences and understand that to do something *new* they must at some point give up something.

Making a change implies heading in a particular direction. As you go north, you travel away from south. To think that you can go somewhere and also remain where you are is not going to work. If the parish chooses to add a worship service that will be more "contemporary," staff and financial resources will be taken away from something else. Something must change. In time, if the new service draws well, it will attract people who may be different from the current members. The new people will change the corporate culture just by their presence. It simply is not possible for everyone in the community to have everything exactly the way he or she wants it all the time. Change has a cost.

When a congregation says, "We want to go boldly into the future," we ask them, "What are you willing to give up in order to do so?"

Start From the Core Values

David Bowie's song "Changes" describes a man trying to turn his reactive changes into proactive change; that is, he wants to gain some control over change rather than being pushed around by it. To do that he must go back to his core values (Bowie says "turned myself to face me"), and he must make some choices about what is important in his life. Change is not easy. A repeated line in "Changes" that you may remember is "Ch-ch-ch-ch-changes (*turn and face the strain*)."

A congregation that wants to become proactive toward change needs to go back to its core values. For example, if the church has a core value of making the Gospel accessible to many people yet is currently having trouble just making it accessible to the people who show up every Sunday, maybe they need to look at *how* the Gospel is presented. Possibly they should consider incorporating artistic media that people are more accustomed to alongside traditional readings and sermons: drama, video clips, poetry, music, more candles, no candles. If conveying the Gospel is a core value and it isn't being conveyed, there needs to be a change.

Since Philip published his book *Ten Dumb Things Churches Do*, people constantly ask him what the number one dumb thing is that churches do. His answer is that many churches are afraid of change.

Jesus said, "Truly I tell you, unless you change and become like children, you will never enter the kingdom of heaven." (Matthew 18:3) We take "being like children" to mean that one must return to a child-like state of total trust in the parent. In a child's trustful world there is no reason to be afraid of change, because our Father/Mother will be there no matter what happens.

"Being like children" also implies a purity of purpose. Children haven't learned how do to one thing when they really prefer to do another. If a child wants to play, he doesn't read a book instead. If a child wants to read a book, she doesn't ride her bicycle instead. While the child's core values may be primitive and his actions undisciplined, there is a direct connection between what the child wants to do, what the child says he wants to do, and what the child actually does. Wouldn't it be wonderful to have that kind of clarity in what we say and do in the church? And to have the trust in God to go with it?

One of the baptismal vows in the Episcopal Church is:

Q. Will you seek and serve Christ in all persons, loving your neighbor as yourself?

A. I will, with God's help.

"Seeking and serving Christ in all persons" means going well beyond hanging a "The Episcopal Church Welcomes You" sign beside the church. As Jesus pointed out in the Parable of the Lost Sheep and the Parable of the Lost Coin, "seeking" means actually going out and looking. Churches that do that kind of seeking are transformed (a fancy word for "changed"), even transfigured (a very fancy word for "changed").

What might happen if we did this? Well, for one thing, there might be considerably more people in the parish hall for the coffee hour. And instead of knowing most or all of the people in the coffee hour, after being transformed, you will know a smaller percentage. God willing, the people you do know will still be there and all of you will be adhering to the Baptismal vow. Change can be fun, as well as being a calling.

If your church's core values won't take you where you sense you are called to go, then it may be time to review the core values. Go back to the second chapter of this book and start with a metaphorical clean sheet of paper. Your core purpose has not changed, but your core values need to be tuned up because you have an overriding value that is your new calling. Any time things do not seem to fit together, it is a good time to "turn and face the strain." Any change means risk, but standing still is a risk, too. Is God calling you to change or not?

Pretty much everything in this book is about learning to overcome fear and trust God. When Jesus walked on the water, Peter wanted to verify that it was actually Jesus out there. So Jesus invited Peter to join him on top of the waves. Peter did all right until his doubts and fears overtook him and he started to sink. And remember what happened then? Jesus lifted him up. Change means stepping out on those waves and almost certainly getting wet, knowing that Jesus will be there to keep us from drowning.

Appendix A

Workshop
Working with Core Theology, "The Big Idea," and Strategic Planning

This outline is intended to assist congregations that are thinking of overhauling their mission statements or engaging in some strategic planning. The outline can be executed by a team on behalf of the congregation, by the whole congregation, or some combination of the two.

Notes: 1) Completing all of the steps outlined will take two or more months for most congregations, and 2) Prayer is an integral part of the process.

Core Theology

1. Begin by reading the chapters on Vision and Corporate Culture (Chapters 2 and 3).

2. Try to write down the church's **stated beliefs** and their sources. For example, the team might note that a core value is belief in "Jesus Christ as Lord and Savior" and that this belief is stated in the baptismal or membership vows.

3. Discuss **actual beliefs** (after establishing that it is safe to do this). This activity is not critical to the process, but it will help refine everyone's understanding of the stated beliefs and open the door to the discussion of operational beliefs that follows.

4. Do your best to name the **operational beliefs**. This may take some time, and it will require wisdom, perspective, and a good sense of humor. It is worthwhile because this process will help in discovering the

corporate culture. We suggest trying this with a small group before engaging the whole congregation in the same process.

a. Begin by listing church activities: worship, Sunday School, Bible study, the men's and women's groups, etc. The list does not need to be exhaustive if this is a large church; six to ten activities should suffice. However, be sure to include the congregation's "big event" if there is one. This might be the annual church fair, book sale, Christmas pageant, etc. This is the kind of event that involves a significant number of the members for two or more months of planning and preparation. It may or may not be a fundraising event. Whatever it is, a truly ongoing "big event" is a key part of the corporate culture of the parish. Also, be sure to include either stewardship or the budget process. Nothing reveals the corporate culture of a parish more than how it handles treasure.

b. Next, begin asking "why" questions about each of the activities (see pp. 59–60). You will need to ask three to five "why" questions for each activity. Each answer will give you an operational belief that could be either a value or a purpose:

> Q: "Why do we hold a Christmas pageant every year?"
>
> A: "We hold the Christmas pageant every year so that the children will learn the Christmas story."

The operational value is that Christian formation is something we want for our children. But don't stop there. Ask *why* we want this for our children.

c. By the end of this process you will have generated between thirty and sixty operational beliefs. Some of them will be the same or similar. Pull them together and see if you can generate a list of five to ten operational beliefs for your congregation.

d. Now compare them to the stated beliefs. How are they similar and how are they different? Write down your conclusions. That should give you some clues to your corporate culture. What would Jesus think of your corporate culture? What do you think of it? The bottom line question is this: does your corporate culture contribute to or detract from your ministry?

5. If you need to bring your operational beliefs more into line with your stated beliefs, brainstorm ways that you might do this short of scaring away most of the congregation. What can you do in worship,

Christian formation, and the budget process that will improve their alignment? Make these items an important part of your strategic plan.

The Big Idea and Strategic Planning

1. Gather ideas

   a. Trends in the parish: Looking at your history, what trends emerge? Going forward, what are the gifts of the parishioners that are likely to be around for a while?

   b. Trends in the context: What is happening in the neighborhood, region, country, judicatory, and denomination?

   c. What can we imagine that may have no connection to either of the two categories above? Think out of the box.
      Allow lots and lots of prayer and silence for this section.

2. Put all of the ideas together:

   a. Is there any overlap?

   b. Where is the energy?

   c. What is the emerging Big Idea, if any?

3. One Big Idea

   a. What would the church look like if you accomplished this?

   b. Note the individual elements of the description.

   c. Pray over the Big Idea for a while and see what other thoughts emerge. *Do not discard it at this point just because is seems "impossible."* Remember that nothing is impossible with God!

4. Strategic Plan

   a. Think about what it will take in the next five years to move towards the Big Idea. Look at the individual elements of the description of the Big Idea and note these as items to place in the strategic plan.

   b. List those smaller ideas that emerged in the gathering stage.

   c. Look at all of the pieces of the strategic plan that you have. Is there something missing? Roof repair? The pastor's retirement?

   d. Refine the pieces of the strategic plan:

      i. Check for overlap and redundancy.

      ii. Set priorities and refine the timeline; some things can be done in the next year; some may take five years or more.

     iii. Check each element against your core beliefs; is there an element that really doesn't belong because it fits only with operational beliefs?

     iv. Assign responsibility for carrying out the plan.

      v. Set up an evaluation mechanism that is done at least annually.

e. Write and publish the core beliefs, the Big Idea, and the strategic plan, and celebrate the ministry to which God is calling you!

Appendix B

Workshop
Hospitality: Becoming a Welcoming Church

The goal of the workshop outlined here is to increase your congregation's awareness of how it welcomes and cares for newcomers and to identify changes that need to be made to put the church in line with the core theology.

This workshop can be done with either a small group of church leaders or as many members of the parish as are interested. Most of the steps are to be done in small groups or even in pairs.

It will be best if the participants have read the chapter on hospitality and even better if they have read the chapter on corporate culture.

As a warm up, you might have the participants watch a scene or two from any of the episodes of *Fawlty Towers*, available on DVD by rental or at public libraries. This sitcom, starring John Cleese and written by John Cleese and Connie Booth, gives a hilarious look at failed hospitality.

Exercises

1. Identify your core theology. What values and beliefs that are operating in the corporate culture of your church encourage or discourage welcoming the stranger?

   a. Start with a key attitude. Does your congregation want to grow? Why? Are you sure?

   b. What would be "enough" growth?

   c. Are you seeking a particular age or ethnic group to expand your congregation? Why?

d. What are you offering? If the church is a "business," what are you "selling"?

2. Bible Study. Genesis 18:1–8—Abraham greets three visitors

a. Put yourself in the story; describe what you "experience"

b. How does the story connect with your church's core theology?

3. "Door slam to door slam." This is an exercise to do on your church campus. In pairs or triads try to see your church from the point-of-view of a first-time visitor. One person should record the observations of the other one or two participants. Begin at the entrance of the parking lot or sidewalk approach to your church and then go inside the church, sit in a pew, and return to the street or parking lot. Ask lots of questions like these:

a. Is there signage that makes it clear where you should go?

b. Is it clear where you are to enter the building?

c. Is there any special accommodation for the first timer?

d. If the main door does not open into the sanctuary, is it clear where you go next when you come in?

e. Are the restrooms easy to find?

f. Is there a table or bulletin board with information visitors would want?

g. When you are done, consider the human element. Do you have greeters in the parking lot? At the front door? At the church entrance? How do you capture information about visitors?

h. Share observations with the whole group.

4. This exercise allows you see your church context in a new way by looking at features of some other institutions, including the reasons people come to them, what kind of hospitality they offer, and the quality of interaction. In small groups discuss the qualities listed for each of the following institutions, plus other qualities the participants can offer. Compare and contrast these with your church.

a. Airport

i. Not the destination

ii. People coming and going; together for a short period

iii. Tries to provide hospitality in the midst of stress

iv. Interaction is low-level

b. Hospital

    i. People come for healing, get well or die, then leave

    ii. Institution provides specific care designed to help people get well

    iii. Hospitality is functional only as relates to healing process

    iv. Interaction is low between patients; high for staff to patient

c. Shrine

    i. People come to see or experience the holy

    ii. Institution may provide high or low level of hospitality

    iii. Interaction may be high or low but is limited to time immediately before and after experience of the holy

d. Club

    i. People select by interest or social quality

    ii. Some procedure for becoming a member

    iii. Some commitment for members

    iv. Institution provides infrastructure to facilitate club function: rules, policies

    v. High interaction for members

e. Summarize your learnings in the whole group

5. Close.

    a. Acknowledge the ways in which your congregation successfully offers hospitality and those areas that need improvement

    b. Consider prayerfully what God may be calling you to do in welcoming the guest.

Notes

1. Richard Giles, *Re-pitching the Tent* (Collegeville, Minn.: Liturgical Press, 1999).

2. San Francisco: Harper and Row, 1973, 95.

3. "Building Your Company's Vision," *Harvard Business Review* (September–October, 1996): 65–77. This article is also available as an OnPoint reprint, product number 410X.

4. Collins and Porras, 66.

5. *The Book of Common Prayer* (New York: Oxford University Press, 1979), 854–55.

6. Rod Reineke and Ruth Wright developed a series of workshops on organizational beliefs from 1992 to 1996 in collaboration with Helene Oswald and Dan Darney. They taught a methodology for opening up conversation among church members or organization employees about the internal values and beliefs that "drive" organizations and may or may not be written down anywhere. This material was never published, but we have found elements of their work very helpful in understanding the subtleties of corporate culture.

7. Anthony B. Robinson, *Transforming Congregational Culture* (Grand Rapids, MI: Wm. B. Eerdmans, 2003), 18 ff.

8. Robinson, 12. The entire second chapter explains clearly the challenge of retrofitting our old institutions to survive in the world today.

9. Robinson, 20–22.

10. Parker J. Palmer, "Leading from Within," *http://www.couragenorthtexas.org/resources/leadingfromwithin.htm.*

11. Adapted from retelling by The Rev. Richard J. Fairchild, www.rockies.net. Original source unknown.

12. King Whitney Jr., quoted in *The Wall Street Journal* (June 7, 1967).